Useless Knowledge

Answers to Questions You'd Never Think to Ask

JOE EDELMAN

The USELESS-Infomaster

and

DAVID SAMSON

UselessKnowledge.com^{SM}

St. Martin's Griffin New York

www.stmartins.com

Book cover design by Biz Stone

Book design by pink design, inc (www.pinkdesigninc.com)

Library of Congress Cataloging-in-Publication Data
Edelman, Joe
  Useless Knowledge : answers to questions you'd never think to ask / Joe Edelman and
David Samson.
    p. cm.
  ISBN 0-312-29017-9
    1. Curiosities and wonders. 2. Questions and answers. I. Samson, David, 1950–. II
Title.
  AG243 .E29 2002
  031.02—dc21

                                                              2002067949

First Edition: September 2002

10 9 8 7 6 5 4 3 2 1

Contents

Introduction

USELESS KNOWLEDGE Replacement Therapy

Thanks to the blessings of the Information Age, our lives are flooded every day by a torrential stream of Useful Information. There's no escape. With the incredible surge of the Internet, cable TV service, satellite dishes, beepers, cell phones, laptops, palm pilots, CD-Roms, DVDs, databanks, downloadable files, video conferencing, webcams, faxes on demand, and of course multiple e-mail addresses, we now officially know more than any other generation that has come before.

Our brains are deluged with facts and figures about global warming, the Nasdaq, NATO, Kosovo, weapons of mass destruction, mad cow disease, and Britney Spears. Small wonder that the use of Prozac and Valium plus dozens of other tranquilizers and antidepressants has skyrocketed to all-time highs—too much information, way too much *Useful* Information! Overloaded by the ceaseless prattle on more than 500 TV channels, plus the lure of a virtually infinite number of Web destinations selling anything from car insurance to Russian wives, the chilling result is that millions of Americans are suffering from RDD—Retention Deficit Disorder!

Luckily, before our minds literally implode from all this pertinent data, there is a way to alleviate the stress—a dynamic course of action that can actually go ahead and help you "delete" the mental clutter that's been oppressing you with the sheer weight of its relevance. That's right. Now you can counter the insidious effects of all this Useful Knowledge and reprogram billions of your brains cells forever! Finally! You can exit the information superhighway and enter the world of…

USELESS KNOWLEDGE!

Never has a book presented so much information that answers questions of so little consequence:

> Which day is National Pecan Day?
> What is a booger made of?
> Do natural blonds have more hairs on their heads than redheads or brunettes?
> Why does the word *pumpernickel* translate to "devil fart"?
> Are there higher decibels when a jet airliner takes off or when a hippopotamus screams during sex?
> Can a passionate kiss burn 6.4 calories per minute?
> Did the U.S. Congress ever pass a law requiring all American citizens to spend one day each year fasting?
> Was murdering a traveling musician considered a serious crime during the Middle Ages?
> Is Waco, Texas, more famous for the death of the Branch Davidians or the birth of Dr Pepper soda?

Let's face it. To call this information irrelevant would be an overstatement!

YOUR BRAIN? *IN PAIN!*

You have a finite amount of brain cells, and what you fill them up with is your business. But according to leading doctors, who by definition have tons of Useful Knowledge they've had to memorize in medical school (such as how to set up judgment-proof corporate accounts in the Cayman Islands), you should be alerted to the fact that if you're capable of reading this paragraph, you are probably losing several billion of these brain cells each second. But don't be alarmed by this—be really, *really* alarmed!

However, your brain cells are not dying because of the aging process or any degenerative disease or your fondness for Dunkin' Donuts. Simply put, they are dying of incredible boredom. They are sick and tired of being eternal repositories of data regarding your mutual fund accounts, the last known location of your golf clubs, the digits of your social security number, your PIN codes, how much you weighed this morning, the names of the people in your carpool, the instructions for setting your VCR, not to mention the exploits of Monica Lewinsky. Let's face it: these cells are withering away on the brain stem, and who can blame them?

A MIND IS A TERRIBLE THING *NOT* TO WASTE

But your brain cells are not just lying around waiting for the blessings of senility. If you keep insisting on taking this course, they will be striking back with a vengeance as long as they have any protoplasm left. Small wonder that Useful Knowledge has been demonstrated to be the leading cause of anxiety, depression, paranoia, schizophrenia, and hives. It's the origin of all stress and insomnia and acute feelings of inadequacy when paying your American Express bill. What's more, Useful Knowledge has also been shown to be a major personality component of individuals who are commonly identified by the rest of us as nerds.

Indeed, this is the most worthless volume you will ever own, which clearly makes it invaluable. Within these pages are chapters that in no way can improve the quality of anyone's life, or we guarantee that person's money back! So if you're looking for tips on how to accumulate wealth, improve your health, change careers, have incredible sex, develop better personal relationships, travel for free, or change your identity, good luck, baby! However, if you're searching for a way to finally eliminate the vast depository of relevant data that's been virtually choking your cerebrum, you've picked up the right handbook—a vast and unimpressive array of meaningless facts, negligible quotes, and 25,000 trifling questions!

So, clearly, it's time to delete all these facts and figures and names and places and get with the program. It's time to reprogram your billions of brain cells with stuff they'll really love—dynamite data that they'll want to keep on file forever and forever and never make you forget. That's right! It's time to replace your lifelong accumulation of Useful Knowledge with USELESS KNOWLEDGE.

THE PROCESS IS MUCH SIMPLER THAN YOU THINK!

This dynamic procedure can and has worked miracles, alleviating migraines, tension, and the annoying realization that no one has invited you to a dinner party for eleven years. Here's how the program works:

Every bit of USELESS KNOWLEDGE you acquire erases immediately and permanently a portion of relevant information in your mind. For example, let's say you're obsessing over the relative number of calories you're ingesting today and even breaking them down by percentage into fats, carbohydrates, and protein to achieve that favorable "balance" of 30-30-40 or whatever, per meal. What a headache! On top of that, try talking about your diet at gallery openings and see how quickly you can alienate half the room (in about three seconds). The only thing more fatigued than your brain cells will be any poor soul within twenty feet of your voice.

Now let's replace that information with something so irrelevant that not only will your gray matter love it, so will anyone else within earshot. For instance:

At a party: "Did you know," you can slyly mention to anyone in earshot, "that a person who is lost in the woods and starving can obtain nourishment by chewing on his shoes. Leather has enough nutritional value to sustain life for a short time."

On a buffet line: instead of debating the merits of the chicken skewers versus the jumbo shrimp with the person next to you, give him or her a great big smile and remark, "Did you know that the stomach must produce a new layer of mucus every two weeks, or it will digest itself?"

On a date: rather than prattling on about what college you went to or your job or the amount of alimony you're paying, just take your date into the kitchen and remove two candles from the refrigerator. Look deeply into his or her stunned eyes and whisper, "Oh, darling, candles burn more slowly and evenly, with minimum wax drippings, if they are placed in the freezer for an hour before using."

With your clients: why put people into a catatonic daze discussing investment strategies or portfolio positioning when you can simply take out your wallet and reveal little nuggets of such as, "I heard that a study of American coins and currency revealed the presence of bacteria, including staphylococcus, and E. coli on 18 percent of the coins and 7 percent of the bills. Has anyone got change for a twenty?"

Over Christmas dinner: just as your mother-in-law is making her royal entrance with her famous honey-suckled ham, blurt out that *the Muppet Show* was banned from TV in Saudi Arabia because one of its stars was a pig.

On politics: shock your audience and bet anyone in the room that John Hanson—and not George Washington—was the first president of the United States. You'll win big time. And finally, if a dispute arises over the major political parties, simply state that you've based your affiliation entirely on the fact that—so far—every U.S. president to have a beard has been a Republican.

There's no doubt about it. When all is said and done, USELESS KNOWLEDGE

Replacement Therapy is the most dynamic, most effective, and of course the cheapest way to improve your mental outlook. It will displace every single one of your highly traumatic experiences, such as the time your mother gave your brother Sidney an extra cookie, and replace them on a cellular level.

That's right: there's no more reason to dredge up your neurotic past during years of expensive analysis, no more need for swallowing costly brain-altering pharmaceuticals, plus you can even cut down on your weekly yoga classes. As a matter of fact, becoming a fountain of USELESS KNOWLEDGE may just be the wisest decision you'll ever make!

A USELESS DISCLAIMER

But exercise caution: the more useless your conversation becomes, the less you have to say of any relevance, the more in demand you will be. Your popularity will skyrocket as you absolutely refuse to discuss anything but the most trivial matters. Hordes of admirers will demand to know the secret of your inconsequential utterances. The sheer unimportance of your words will make them resonate far and wide.

Devotees will listen attentively as you state that your favorite animal is the "zeedonk" (the offspring of a zebra and a donkey), or why the most intriguing woman in history has to be Anne Boleyn, Henry VIII's second wife, who wore special gloves to hide her six-fingered hand. You might also add that she had three breasts.

Best of all, unlike Useful Knowledge, which has a shelf life of about fifteen minutes, USELESS KNOWLEDGE never has to be updated, modified, changed, defended, or ever retracted. Which means USELESS KNOWLEDGE never becomes obsolete. It never goes out of style. It's just as useless today as it was yesterday and will be tomorrow. That's right: you couldn't possibly ask for a more worthless guarantee. And truthfully, the more you think about it, who could ask for anything less?

Course Catalog:
The College of USELESS KNOWLEDGE:

A Complete Curricum of Absolutely NO Value

Unfortunately, most of the really damaging Useful Knowledge you acquired was in school, with the sabotage starting in kindergarten and continuing (for some of you) right through the graduate level of education. Therefore, to undo all these years of cerebral abuse, we have structured our own unique college curriculum. Facts your teachers should have taught you long ago, but didn't because they were too preoccupied with making sure that you became a productive member of society. Well, rest assured, we have no such wish.

To prove that, we've made the College of USELESS KNOWLEDGE into a revolutionary center of *unlearning*. We offer no lectures, no discussions, no credits, no tuition, no classes, no professors, no majors, no admission requirements, no attendance requirements, no graduation requirements—nothing. Our courses are easy because you never have to study. Just peruse the points contained in each area, and you instantly qualify for a Useless Degree in that area. Of course, it'll probably be just as useless as the degree you have now, but it will be a lot more fun to get!

From the ironic to the moronic, gorge yourself on trivial facts, quotes, strange customs, quizzes, celebrity stats, obscure sports and historical data, inconsequential biographies and birthdays. Guzzle up truly wacky aspects of sex, love, politics, relationships, animals, diet, exercise, criminals, beasts, science, technology, and much more. Virtually unknown and startling data will lure you back to complete one course of study after another, until you become a totally Useless Scholar, a prestigious member of the nonacademic community, possessing a proud education second to all!

Well, what are you waiting for? Whether you chose to attend one of our major schools or their institutes, the semester is about to begin!

1

The USELESS
School of
World History

It's true. No matter how many important names or dates you've memorized, Useless History Replacement Therapy works wonders at eliminating all of them.

You've heard about the lost continent of Atlantis, but how about the lost state of Franklin? It was formed just after the American Revolution in 1784. It elected a governor, levied taxes, and enacted laws, but now it's been forgotten. Which is good—because this chapter is full of stuff that should be forgotten! Sure, everybody remembers that Thomas Edison invented the modern lightbulb—but hey, what about the inventor of the modern flush toilet? It was none other than Thomas Crapper.

War buffs will appreciate the fact that Hitler had a square mustache—because his favorite comedian, Charlie Chaplin, had a square mustache. Even Colin Powell may not know that the shortest conflict on record was not the Gulf War, but the war between Britain and Zanzibar in 1896, which lasted just 38 minutes.

Oh, yes, if you've got snotty friends who attended Harvard or Yale, now tell them what cheap schools they actually went to. When Elihu Yale donated $2,500 to the Collegiate School, its name suddenly became Yale University. And when John Harvard contributed $3,500 and a little library to Cambridge College, it immediately mutated into Harvard University. That's right: history is filled with important lessons and dates. Hopefully, we've avoided all of them!

A survey disclosed that 12 percent of Americans believe that Joan of Arc was Noah's wife. Hopefully, you're not one of them!

Course 101: **Rome and the Caesar Salad**

> The word *trivia* derives from the Latin *tri* + *via*, which translates as "three streets." As a major public service in Roman times, at the intersection of three streets, there was a kind of kiosk where further info was posted for travelers. Apparently these data were so useless that citizens often ignored them entirely: thus, they were truly bits of "trivia."
> In Rome, the world's first paved streets were laid out in 170 B.C. The new streets were popular, as they were functional in all types of weather and were easy to keep clean, but they amplified the city's noise level.
> Julius Caesar banned all wheeled vehicles from Rome during daylight hours because of heavy traffic congestion.

Roman gladiators, as a result of their immense public appeal, gave commercial product endorsements.

> The Roman emperor Nero married his male slave Sporus in a public cere-mony, while Emperor Caligula was so proud of his horse that he gave the animal a place as a senate consul before he died!

> Thousands of years before the WWF, the emperor Commodus gathered all the dwarfs, cripples, and freaks his guards could locate around Rome and had them dragged over to the Colosseum. There they were all given meat cleavers and commanded to hack each other to death.

Roman statues were made with detachable heads, so that one head could be removed and replaced by another.

> The word *decimate* came into being from motivational techniques employed by Roman commanders. Whenever a legion performed dismally during combat, every tenth soldier was killed. The Latin for this process is *decimare*, stemming from *decimus*, or "tenth."

> In the Roman Republic of 500 B.C., the senate could appoint a supreme national commander for a limited time during periods of emergency. While in charge, his word was law. His title in Latin meant "I have spoken." The title was "dictator."

From the early Roman Empire until eighteenth-century Europe and America, urine was a main ingredient in toothpaste, because the ammonia in it is an excellent cleaner. Ammonia is still a main ingredient in many types of toothpaste.

> The word *testimony* came from men in Roman times taking an oath before the court that they were telling the truth. To insure their statements were accurate, they swore on their testicles.

While Rome ruled the world, Jesus Christ, son of Mary, was born in a cave, not in a wooden stable. Caves were used to house animals because they retained heat. A large church is now built over the cave, and people can go inside. The carpenters of Jesus' day were really stonecutters as wood was not used as widely as it is today. So whenever you see a Christmas nativity scene with a wooden stable, that's the "American" version, not the Biblical one.

GETTING THE LEAD OUT

Lead poisoning has been blamed for contributing to the fall of the Roman Empire. Women became infertile by drinking wine from vessels whose lead had dissolved in the wine, and the Roman upper classes died out within a couple centuries. The Romans used lead as a sweetening agent and as a cure for diarrhea. It added up to massive self-inflicted poisoning.

Course 107: **Mummy Dearest**

> The exalted pharaoh Ramses II fathered over 160 kids. To immortalize this achievement, the Ramses brand of condoms bears his name.

> Cleopatra was part Macedonian, part Greek, and part Iranian. She was not Egyptian.

> In ancient Egypt, when a woman's husband was convicted of a crime, she and her children were punished as well. They were usually enslaved.

The bandaging of a mummy took from 6 to 8 months. It required a collection of special tools, including a long metal hook that was used to draw the dead person's brains out through his nose.

> One of the Seven Wonders of the Ancient World was a lighthouse, the famous Pharos of Alexandria in Egypt. Pharos was the first lighthouse in history, and is still the tallest on record. (It was 450 feet high—about the size of a 45-story skyscraper.)

> Ancient robbers of Egyptian tombs were convinced that whacking off the noses of stone effigies would thwart any nasty curses.

> Better than Minoxydil? According to Greek historian Herodotus, Egyptian men never became bald. The reason was that, as children, males had their heads shaved, and their scalps were continually exposed to the health-giving rays of the sun.

The ancient Egyptians worshiped a sky goddess called Nut.

> In 1500 B.C. in Egypt, a shaved head was considered the ultimate in feminine beauty. Egyptian women removed every hair from their heads with special gold tweezers and polished their scalps to a high sheen with buffing cloths.

> In ancient Egypt, when merchants left the country on business trips, they carried small stone models of themselves. If they died while abroad, these figures were sent back to Egypt for proxy burial. Considering the cost of present-day funerals, this seems like a pretty good idea!

Birth-control campaigns in Egypt in the late 1970s failed because village women ended up wearing the pills in lockets, as talismans.

IT'S A WRAP!

Although the early Egyptians were the most famous mummy makers, they were not exactly the first to practice this now-long-dead art. An extremely advanced fishing tribe known as the Chinchoros, who inhabited the north coast of what is present-day Chile, were wrapping up their ex-tribesmen from head to toe as early as 5000 B.C.— way before the pharoahs!

Course 118: **It's Greek to Me**

> In ancient Greece, prostitutes wore sandals with nails studded into the soles so that their footprints would leave the message "Follow me."

> Florida officials should take note: officials of ancient Greece decreed that mollusk shells be used as ballots, because once a vote was scratched on the shell, it couldn't be erased or altered.

> A temple of Aphrodite, the Greek goddess of love, was discovered coincidentally by American archaeologist Iris C. Love.

Groundhog Day owes its true origins to the ancient Greeks, who believed that an animal's shadow was its soul, blackened by the past year's sins. While the animal hibernates, its soul is cleansed by nature, and if it wakes up before winter is over, it will see the dirty shadow and be horrified and then return to its den for more purification.

> In ancient Greece, women counted their age from the date on which they were married, not from the date of their birth—a tradition many women appear to follow today.

> Oddly, in ancient Greece no term existed for *homosexuality*—there were only some expressions referring to specific homosexual roles. Experts find this baffling, as the old Greek culture held love between males in the highest regard. According to several linguists, the word *homosexual* was not coined until 1869 by the Hungarian physician Karoly Maria Benkert.

Greek conqueror Alexander the Great ordered his entire army to shave their faces and heads. He believed beards and long hair were too easy for an enemy to grab in order to decapitate his victim.

THE TALIBAN WOULD HAVE APPROVED

Married women were forbidden by law to watch, let alone compete, in the ancient Olympics. The Greeks believed that the presence of wives in Olympia would defile Greece's oldest religious shrine, which was located there. However, young maidens were allowed to attend. Any married woman who dared break the rule was thrown from a nearby cliff to her death.

Ironically, the shrine that was off-limits to married women was dedicated to a woman, the fertility goddess Rhea, who was mother of the supreme god, Zeus.

Course 192: **Medieval (or Just Evil) Times**

> After his death in 896, the body of Pope Formosus was dug up and tried for various crimes.

> During the Renaissance artists could not depict woman's toes or bare feet in their paintings. This way, they were spared any "callous" remarks from critics.

Renaissance artist Michelangelo's last name was Buonarroti, which he obviously never used.

> The men who served as guards along the Great Wall of China in the Middle Ages often were born on the wall, grew up there, married there, died there, and were buried within it. Many of these guards never left the wall in their entire lives.

> Much like today, in the Middle Ages, no one really trusted anyone else. As someone approached, to alleviate paranoia, he would hold out his open palm to show that he was not going to whack your head off with a sword. This gesture put everybody at ease, and eventually evolved into the modern custom known as the handshake.

> Back in the 1600s, thermometers were filled with brandy instead of mercury.

> The dread Black Plague in Europe was partially due to the belief that people thought cats were witches. Therefore, all the felines were hauled away and incinerated, which left the rats (who hosted the true culprits: plague-breeding fleas) to run around towns and villages and multiply. Ironically, cat lovers giving felines safe haven were a large part of those who survived.

> It is thought that the saying "pulling your leg" originated from the custom in the Middle Ages of hanging people in such a creative way that the victims often choked slowly and in agony. To put an end to their sufferings, pals or relatives of the suffocating victims would pull down hard on their legs in order to snap their necks.

In the sixteenth and seventeenth centuries, some people thought comets were the eggs or sperm of planetary systems.

> In Peking, during the Middle Ages, one took revenge against one's enemies by placing finely chopped tiger whiskers in their food. The whisker barbs would get caught in the victim's digestive tract and cause sores and infections. Not even the earliest forms of Pepto Bismal helped!

> When medieval clans wanted to downsize and dispose of unwanted folks without murdering them, they just burned their houses to the ground as a small hint. Thus the phrase "to get fired."

Public sanitation was at an all-time low during the Middle Ages. Garbage was piled up so high outside the city of Paris during the 1400s that it interfered with the city's defenses.

> In feudal Japan, the Imperial army had special soldiers whose only duty was to count the number of severed enemy heads after each battle. And if they came up with the wrong amount, heads would definitely roll!

During the Middle Ages, murdering a traveling musician was not considered a serious crime.

WOULD JERRY FALWELL APPROVE?

During the fifteenth century, Venice ordained that local Italian prostitutes should bare their breasts while soliciting at open windows overlooking the city's famous canals and walkways. The ruling was intended to separate the city's "professional" women from the general citizens, and also to encourage young men to purchase the prostitutes' wares and avoid the unspeakable sins of masturbation and homosexuality.

Course 158: **Chris and Friends Set Sail**

> Everybody knows that the first Spanish vessels to reach the New World were commanded by the Italian Christoforo Colombo (no relation to Peter Falk). But what about other nations? The first English vessels to reach the New World were commanded by the Italian Giovanni Caboto (John Cabot), and the first French vessels were commanded by the Italian Giovanni da Verrazano.
> The first gold brought back by Christopher Columbus from the Americas was used to gild the ceiling of the Church of Santa Maria Maggiore in Rome. The ceiling and the gold are still there today.
> Christopher Columbus had blond hair.
> The Caribbean island of Nevis once issued a postage stamp depicting Christopher Columbus peering into a telescope. However, Columbus sailed to the Americas in 1492; the telescope wasn't invented until 1608.

Course 162: **Ooh-La-La!**

> In 1418, women's headgear was so tall that, on the orders of the queen, the doorways of the royal castle of Vincennes, France, were raised to allow the ladies of the court to pass through without ducking.
> In the court of French King Louis XI, the fine ladies lived mainly on soup because they believed that excessive chewing would cause them to develop premature facial wrinkles.

> Toward the latter part of the fifteenth century, men's footwear had a square tip resembling a duck's beak, a fashion trend started by Charles VIII to hide the deformity of one of his feet, which had an extra toe.

The shallow champagne glass originated with Marie Antoinette, from wax molds made of her breasts.

> Not that he was immature, but Napoleon concocted his battle strategies in a sandbox.
> In France, Napoleon instituted a scale of fines for sex offenses that included 35 francs for a man guilty of lifting a woman's skirt to the knee and 75 francs if he lifted it to the thigh.
> Napoleon Bonaparte was always depicted with his hand inside his jacket because he suffered from "chronic nervous itching" and often scratched his stomach sores until they bled.

One of Napoleon's drinking cups was made from the skull of the famous Italian adventurer Cagliostro.

Where's the Can Opener?

Napoleon appointed three scientists to create a device that would preserve rations for his troops as they attacked Russia. Their brainchild: canned food. In the French team was Louis Pasteur, the inventor of the pasteurization method. The technique they developed for canning is virtually the same process used today. Unfortunately, the scientists didn't also invent a can opener. So by relying on knives and bayonets to pierce the thick metal cans, many soldiers severely wounded themselves, some even cutting off a finger or two!

> Dentistry in eighteenth-century Paris was horribly barbaric. Louis XIV had teeth pulled so roughly by an overzealous dentist that when he tried to drink his soup, it cascaded out of his nose.

Sculptor Frederic-Auguste Bartholdi of France originally named his most famous work *Liberty Enlightening the World*. Bartholdi used his mother as the model for the statue's face—and his girlfriend as the model for her body. Smart!

Course 150: **Those Crazy Colonials!**

> Contrary to popular belief, Daniel Boone reportedly did not like coonskin caps.
> Do you think that the Vietnam War had a lot of draft dodgers? Only 16 percent of the able-bodied males in the thirteen original American colonies participated in the Revolutionary War.
> The name of the Pilgrims' second ship was the *Speedwell*. However, unlike the *Mayflower*, it had to turn back because it wasn't seaworthy.
> The typical woman living in seventeenth-century America gave birth to 13 youngsters. Benjamin Franklin, born in 1706, was his mom's 16th kid.

Benjamin Franklin was the proud owner of the very first bathtub in the colonies.

> Ben Franklin wanted the turkey, not the eagle, to be the U.S. national symbol. He considered the eagle a "bird of bad moral character" because it lives "by sharping and robbing."
> Benjamin Franklin slept in four beds every night. He had a theory that a warm bed sapped a man's vitality. So when one bed became too warm, Ben jumped into another.

John Hanson—not George Washington—was legally the first president of the United States. When Congress met in 1781, the country was governed by the Articles of Confederation, which were adopted in 1777 and ratified by the states in 1781. At that meeting, Congress elected John Hanson its "President of the U.S. in Congress assembled." After that, George Washington became the first president of the country under the U.S. Constitution in 1789.

> When delivering his famous "Farewell Address," Washington spoke through false teeth that were fashioned from whalebone.
> Speaking of choppers, Betsy Ross, the woman who designed and sewed the first American flag, had a completely developed set of teeth at birth.
> Betsy Ross also ran a munitions factory from her basement. Yet her biggest claim to fame may be that she is one of the only real people along with Daniel Boone, ever to be immortalized as a Pez head.

The Pilgrims did not build log cabins, nor did they wear black hats with a conical crown and a hatband with a silver buckle.

> Some things never change: Cutouts of a moon and a star were used in colonial times on outhouse doors to designate the gender of the intended user.

Originally, the moon cutout was for women, and the star was for the men. But men's outhouses were such a mess that men preferred using the women's outhouses. So, eventually the use of stars were phased out.

> During his midnight ride on April 18, 1775, Paul Revere did not shout, "The British are coming." Instead, his call was "The regulars are coming." The regulars were the British troops. Apparently, you could be considered "regular" in those days even if you were a constipated Brit.
> During the War of Independence, more inhabitants of the American colonies fought for the British than for the Continental Army.

Both Goldie Hawn and Tom Hanks are fond of their privates: *Private Benjamin* and *Saving Private Ryan*, respectively. However, they also share patriotic pedigrees. Tom Hanks is a descendant of Nancy Hanks, Abraham Lincoln's mother, while Goldie Hawn's father, Edward Rutledge Hawn, is a descendant of a signer of the Declaration of Independence.

> The people we call Pennsylvania Dutch originally came from Germany—not Holland. "Dutch" comes from the word *Deutsch*, meaning German.
> In the Declaration of Independence as first written by Thomas Jefferson, there was a clause abolishing slavery. However, because of pressure, he was forced to delete the clause.
> Lotteries are not new. The original thirteen colonies of the United States were financed with the help of lottery dollars. Additionally, the U.S. government used lotteries to raise money to help defray the costs of the Revolutionary and Civil Wars.
> When it came time to build the Capitol building, a contest was held to see who the designer would be. The winner was William Thornton, a doctor and amateur architect, who received $500 and a city lot as his prize.

When Thomas Jefferson became president in 1801, 20 percent of all people in the young nation were slaves. The population was 5 million people in all, making for 1 million slaves.

BEFORE ALCOHOLICS ANONYMOUS...

The delegates who attended the Constitutional Convention spent much of their time getting drunk. One surviving document is a bill for a party on September 15, 1787, two days before the signing of the Constitution. Items on the bill were: 54 bottles of Madeira, 60 bottles of claret, 8 bottles of whiskey, 22 bottles of cider, 12 bottles of beer, and 7 bowls of alcoholic punch, all for 55 people. Talk about a political party!

Course 144: **Stylish History**

> Around 1400 B.C., it was the fashion among rich Egyptian women to place a large cone of scented grease on top of their heads. As the day wore on, it melted and dripped down their bodies, covering their skin with an oily, glistening sheen and bathing their clothes in fragrance.

> Early Roman fashion designers combined the Greek *perzoma*, the first fabricated underwear, and the Etruscan *succinta*, a belt, and produced the bikini for use by athletes. Little did they realize their innovation would one day revolutionize swimwear, plus boost sales of *Sports Illustrated*.

Piercing isn't some new punk fad. From earliest times, people pierced their ears, nose, nipples, and navel, as the holes produced were thought to release demons from the body.

> In the 1400s, a popular form of shoes called "crakows" sported extremely long toes. The length of the toes, which could measure over 20 inches, was an indication of the social status of the person wearing them.

> In England, laws were passed that prescribed which fashions could not be worn by the lower classes, so as to keep social distinctions intact. Queen Elizabeth would not allow the neck ruff to be worn by the riff-raff.

Catherine the Great of Russia kept her wig maker in an iron cage in her bedroom for more than three years.

> During the rule of Peter the Great, any Russian man who wore a beard was required to pay a special tax, although you could get away scot-free with just a mustache and sideburns.

In the fifteenth century, special laws were decreed to ensure that the handkerchief was allowed only to the nobility, since they were generally snots.

> In ancient times, the traditional color of bridal gowns was red. The wife of Napoleon III broke the tradition and wore a white gown. Then, brides began wearing white gowns (which were worn only once) as a symbol of their wealth.

> *Chopines* were platform shoes that became popular in Europe during the sixteenth century. Some *chopines* were over twenty inches tall.

Fashionable ladies of the sixteenth century thought it elegant to allow their pubic hair to grow as lengthy as possible. This way, it could be braided, pomaded, and embellished with bows and ribbons.

> During the Renaissance, blondes definitely had more fun. Blond hair for women became so much de rigueur in Venice that a brunette was not to be seen except among the working classes. Venetian women spent hours dyeing and burnishing their hair until they achieved the harsh metallic glitter that was considered a necessity.

Well-dressed ladies in Europe went wild over wearing lightning rods on their hats and trailing a long ground wire—a fad that began after Benjamin Franklin published instructions on how to make them in his almanac *Poor Richard Improved* in 1753.

Course 145: **The British Empire (Not!)**

> The good news in 1547 in Britain was that the law was amended to end the practice of boiling criminals to death. The bad news was that the punishment was changed to burning them at the stake.
> In 1789, burning was banned, and the law was altered to make the preferred method of execution hanging. But in any event, as an added measure of cruelty, the prisoner's last meal always consisted of British food.

Soap was considered a frivolous luxury of the British aristocracy from the early 1700s until 1862, and there was a tax on those who used it in England. Today it is apparently a frivolous luxury only for the French.

> The first lighthouse in England was built in 1619 at the Lizard, Cornwall. Legend suggests that the man who built it, Sir John Killigrew, was actually a pirate and wanted to lure ships close to the shore to plunder them.
> The average life span of London residents in the middle of the nineteenth century was 27 years. For members of the working class, it was 22 years.
> Berengaria, queen of England and wife of Richard the Lionhearted, never set foot in England. She lived in Italy most of her life while her husband was off on adventures and crusades.

Henry VIII's second wife, Anne Boleyn, had six fingers on one hand. She wore special gloves all her life to hide her deformity. She also had three breasts.

> In 1664, Maryland passed the first law forbidding English women to marry black men. Any white woman marrying a black slave would herself become a slave until her husband died. However, the edict never declared what would happen to any white guy who married a black woman. Hmm...
> Citizens of seventeenth-century England used ashes, bread, and urine to clean their clothes.

> It has been declared by Parliament that sending a letter with a postage stamp bearing the likeness of the queen (or king) is an act of treason if the stamp is stuck on upside down.
> The first Jewish member of the British House of Commons was Lionel Nathan Rothschild, of the prominent family of European bankers. He did not assume his seat for eleven years, until Parliament finally let him take the oath in a manner acceptable to his Jewish faith.

You can call it Britain, Great Britain, the United Kingdom, or the U.K.—but if you purchase a stamp there, you won't find its name. Great Britain was the first country in the world to issue postage stamps—and it's the only nation in the world today that doesn't use a national name on its stamps.

Course 179: **The Civil or Uncivil War?**

> The Supreme Court once ruled the Federal income tax unconstitutional. Income tax was first imposed during the Civil War as a temporary revenue-raising measure. Try telling that to the IRS!
> Dr. Samuel A. Mudd treated the leg of Abraham Lincoln's assassin, John Wilkes Booth. His actions produced the expression "his name is Mudd," signifying utter disgrace.
> Before all-porcelain teeth were perfected in the mid nineteenth century, dentures were commonly made with teeth pulled from the mouths of dead soldiers following a battle. Teeth extracted from the cadavers of U.S. Civil War soldiers were shipped to English dentists by the barrel.
> Before the Civil War, the United States offered the highly respected Robert E. Lee the position of commander of the Union forces. He declined.

On his way home to visit his parents, a Harvard student fell between two railroad cars at the station in Jersey City, New Jersey, and was rescued by an actor on his way to visit a sister in Philadelphia.

The student was Robert Lincoln, heading for 1600 Pennsylvania Avenue. The actor was Edwin Booth, the brother of the man who a few weeks later would murder the student's father.

> The expression "it's so cold out there it could freeze the balls off a brass monkey" derived from the Civil War. To stack up cannonballs, they were placed into a pyramid formation known as a brass monkey. But when the weather got frigid outside, they would fracture and split off...thus the popular aphorism.

> By the end of the Civil War, 33 percent of all paper currency in circulation was counterfeit. So on July 5, 1865, the Secret Service was created as a part of the Department of the Treasury to help suppress counterfeit currency.

The first graves in Arlington National Cemetery were dug by James Parks, a former Arlington Estate slave. Buried in Section 15, James Parks is the only person buried in Arlington National Cemetery who was also born on the property.

> Hookers got their title during the Civil War, when Gen. Joseph Hooker, of the Union Army, tried to boost morale by allowing prostitutes access to his troops. Quickly dubbed "Hooker's girls," the prostitutes shortened the name to "hookers." The term stuck.
> Gen. George Armstrong Custer graduated at the bottom of his West Point class in 1861.
> George Armstrong Custer's younger brother, Thomas Custer, was the only soldier to win two Congressional Medals of Honor during the Civil War. He joined his older brother's regiment and also died at Little Bighorn.

The first woman executed by the U.S. government was Mary Surratt. She was hanged July 7, 1865, for conspiracy in the assassination of President Lincoln.

> While Jefferson Davis, president of the Confederacy, was secretary of war in the U.S. cabinet, he expanded the size of the armed forces, allowed the implementation of a new rifle musket, and fashioned other military advances. But all these achievements came back to haunt him. For later they helped contribute to the obliteration of the Confederacy.
> Sarah Edmonds was one of many women who fought in the U.S. Civil War in disguise as a man. She became a Union spy, and later deserted to protect her secret. Edmonds revealed her true identity after the war in an attempt to clear herself of the desertion charges and gain a pension.

Confederate general Robert E. Lee's boots had to be removed in order for him to be stuffed into his undersized coffin.

> During the nineteenth century, Michigan was a key stop on the Underground Railroad, and many runaway slaves decided to make their homes there. Currently, 14 percent of Michigan's population is African-American.
> When the Civil War ended, the United States sued England for damages resulting from its construction of ships for the Confederacy. America initially demanded $1 billion in payment, but eventually settled for just $25 million. History doesn't record whether the British check was certified or not.

Kennedy was the name of a secretary who worked for Abraham Lincoln, while strangely enough, Lincoln was the name of a secretary who worked for John F. Kennedy.

Course 162: World War II

> Sadly, when the Allies dropped their very first bomb on Berlin, it wound up landing right in the Berlin Zoo, instantly killing the Nazis' only elephant.
> During World War II, on January 18, 1943, bakers in the United States were ordered to stop selling sliced bread for the duration of the war. Only whole loaves were made available to the public. It was never explained how this action helped the war effort.

The British royal family changed their last name to Windsor from Saxe-Coburg-Gotha during World War I so as not to appear pro-German. They have never changed it back.

> During World War II, the Japanese used shark liver oil in the engines of their fighter planes—and not one of those planes ever developed cancer!
> While World War II was being fought, the original copies of the U.S. Constitution and the Declaration of Independence were taken from the Library of Congress and kept at Fort Knox, Kentucky.
> The Germans considered *Casablanca* (1943) a propaganda film and made it illegal to show it in German theaters during World War II. Even after the war, only a censored version was allowed to be shown in Germany; all references to Nazis were removed.

THE CODE TALKERS

Peter MacDonald, former leader of the Navajo nation, was one of the famed Navajos used by the U.S. military during World War II to stump the Japanese by using their native tongue as a communications code. In a Texas medical prison since 1992, at age 72, he was pardoned on President Clinton's last day in office in 2001. He'd been sentenced for his role in a Window Rock, Arizona, riot that killed two people in 1989.

> In the midst of World War II, the U.S. Navy's world champion chess player, Reuben Fine, calculated, on the basis of positional probability, where enemy submarines might surface. Although Fine was merely a pawn, he helped "checkmate" the enemy.
> During World War II, the free-tailed bat caves near San Antonio were guarded closely as part of top-secret Operation X-ray. The U.S. military attempted to

train the bats to carry small incendiary bombs and release them in Japanese buildings. During one test, bat bomb carriers escaped and set fire to barracks and a general's car. The project was later scrapped.

The parents of Dwight D. Eisenhower—commander of Allied Forces, who rose to become one of the few five-star generals in U.S. history—were pacifists.

> The phrase "the whole 9 yards" derives from World War II combat pilots in the South Pacific. Their planes were armed with machine guns that took .50 caliber ammo belts, which were exactly 27 feet long. Hence, whenever the pilots blasted all their bullets at a target, it caught "the whole 9 yards."
> Among the first Americans to join the Royal Air Force and help in the Battle of Britain was "Shorty" Keough. At 4' 10" tall, he was the shortest pilot in the RAF, requiring several cushions to see out of his cockpit.

The Studebaker auto company produced a car called the Dictator from 1927–36. However, Hitler didn't own one, as far as we know.

> During World War II, the Revlon company reinforced the war effort by producing dye markers for the U.S. Navy. Whether any of the same dye subsequently went into waterproof mascara, no one can say.
> Television broadcasts were suspended until the end of World War II in 1945. This delayed the development of an affordable television system until the late 1940s.
> During World War II, guards were posted at the fence of the White House. Before that, anyone could wander right up to the front door.

During World War II, in May 1942, U.S. ice cream manufacturers were restricted by law to produce only 20 different flavors of ice cream. But to this date, no explanation for the law has ever been offered.

> Right after World War II, a pinup photo of actress Rita Hayworth adorned the first test A-bomb, dropped on Bikini Atoll in the Marshall Islands in July 1946. Rita was a real bombshell!
> When Albert Einstein escaped Germany in 1933, the Nazis put a price of 20,000 marks on his head. The price was never marked down!

In 1944, Maj. Clark Gable's army discharge papers were signed by President-to-be Ronald Reagan, then a captain.

> Adolf Hitler's favorite dog, Blondi, an Alsatian, was used to make sure his cyanide capsules were lethal. Hitler used the cyanide to commit suicide when he saw it worked on Blondi.

Shockingly enough, Hitler was voted *Time* magazine's Man of the Year in 1938. Now how did Osama ever miss?

HONORS COURSE: JAPANESE-AMERICAN PATRIOTS

The most decorated outfit in the history of the U.S. military consisted almost entirely of enlistees from the World War II–period internment camps for citizens of Japanese-American descent. Despite being herded into these camps, the vast majority wanted to prove their patriotism. Their outfit was given the nicknames of the "Go-for-Broke Brigade" and the "Purple Heart Battalion." Among the brave fighters was Daniel Inouye, who later became a distinguished senator from Hawaii.

Final Exam

1. In A.D. 700, the largest city in the Americas was located almost exactly where Hoboken, New Jersey, stands today.   **True or False?**

2. In ancient China, people committed suicide by eating a pound of flesh.   **True or False?**

3. Pocahontas appeared on the back of the $20 bill in 1875.   **True or False?**

4. Armored knights lifted their visors when they rode past their king so that he would recognize them. This tradition has evolved into the present-day military salute.   **True or False?**

5. The expression "rule of thumb" originated from an old British law that decreed that a man could not beat his wife with any object wider than his thumb.   **True or False?**

6. In 1502, on his fourth journey to America, Christopher Columbus became the first European to taste roasted turkey.   **True or False?**

7. One penalty for an unfaithful wife in medieval France was to force her to pursue a chicken through the village naked.

True or False?

8. Robert Todd Lincoln, the son of Abraham Lincoln, was in proximity during his life to a total of three presidential assassinations: those of Lincoln, Garfield, and Kennedy.

True or False?

9. In the early 1700s, a special Witchcraft Act identified beavers as dangerous animals to be shunned.

True or False?

10. In 1776, at the time of the Revolution, Americans had the lowest standard of living and the highest taxes in all of the Western World.

True or False?

ANSWERS

1. FALSE: It was Teotihuacán, located in central Mexico. The city belonged to the Mayan civilization and was home to over 100,000 people and 600 pyramids.

2. FALSE: They swallowed a pound of salt.

3, 4, and 5. TRUE.

6. FALSE: He tasted chocolate.

7. TRUE.

8. FALSE: It was McKinley, not Kennedy.

9. FALSE: The law warned against black cats, not beavers.

10. FALSE: Actually, they had the highest standard of living and the lowest taxes. Go figure!

2

The USELESS
School of
Animals

Featuring the Useless Insect Institute

Sure, you can tell the difference between a cocker spaniel and a Labrador retriever, but do you know what's really different about a Doberman? Well, there was actually a guy called Doberman. It turns out he lived in Germany back in the 1880s, but was rather disdained by the local townsfolk since he was also the tax collector. So Doberman bred a special type of dog to accompany him on his rounds. Get the picture?

Now let's turn our attention to creatures of the wild, like tigers. You know they have striped fur—but did you realize they also have striped skin beneath that fur? Many people are aware that bats hang upside down in caves all day and that they come out at night. So what else is new? It just so happens that when they exit those caves, they invariably turn left—and probably without signaling, either!

All right. What about elephants? You know everything about their large trunks, but what about their penises? The elephant has the largest penis in the animal kingdom—even without Viagra. It may extend as far as 6 feet (that's feet!) and weigh about 60 pounds. On the other hand, when that gigantic gorilla in the zoo looks ferociously at you, it could just be showing penis envy, since its paltry appendage is only two-thirds the length of a human male penis and as thin as a pencil.

So clearly, when it comes to the fascinating and fabulously diverse world of animals, you're totally uninformed. But don't worry, that beastly state is about to be cured with Useless Animal Replacement Therapy!

Course 203: **Compared to Humans**

> A shrimp has more than 100 pairs of chromosomes in each cell nucleus. Man has only twenty-three—even guys who really *are* shrimps.
> Although only 9 inches tall, an adult roadrunner can keep pace with a human sprinter.
> Though human noses have an impressive 5 million olfactory cells with which to smell, sheepdogs have 220 million, enabling them to smell 44 times better than men.
> A bird sees everything at once in total focus. Whereas the human eye is globular and must adjust to varying distances, the bird's eye is flat and can take in everything at once in a single glance.

The leech has 32 brains—31 more than a human.

> A dolphin's flipper has 5 digits and nearly the same bone structure as a human arm and hand.
> A dolphin produces notes 100 times higher than the highest note a human soprano can reach—even in the shower.

> Pigs, dogs, and some other animals can taste water, but people cannot. Humans don't actually taste water or even Perrier; they taste the chemicals and impurities in the water.

Koalas and humans are the only animals with unique finger-prints. Koala prints cannot be distinguished from human fingerprints. Luckily, few koalas pursue a life of crime.

> The sperm whale has the biggest brain of any mammal. Its brain weighs up to 20 pounds, while the human brain weighs 3 pounds.
> While humans are 15 times larger than the common cat, the human skeleton has only 206 bones. Housecats have 230 bones.
> The squirrel monkey's brain accounts for roughly 5 percent of its body weight—the largest percentage of any animal. The human brain, by comparison, makes up about 2.3 percent of body weight.

Unlike humans, the oyster is usually ambisexual. It begins life as a male, then becomes a female, then changes back to being a male, then back to female. It may go back and forth many times—and without paying for an operation, either!

Course 208: **Going to the Dogs**

> The expression *three dog night* originated with the Eskimos and means a very cold night—so cold that you have to bed down with three dogs to keep warm.
> Contrary to popular belief, dogs do not sweat by salivating. They sweat through the pads of their feet.
> Dogs that do not tolerate small children well are the St. Bernard, the Old English sheepdog, the Alaskan malamute, the bull terrier, and the toy poodle. So now you know what to get your obnoxious nephew as a pet.
> Every hour, nearly 12,500 puppies are born in the United States, and there are over 1 million stray dogs living in the New York City metropolitan area alone.

Annually in China, over 100,000 Saint Bernards are slaugh-tered—and served as gourmet dishes in restaurants. The number of Pekingese poodles that become entrées has not been reported.

> A sexually aroused feline may attempt to seduce a dog; that canine becomes the cat's meow, so to speak.

> The seeing-eye dog, or any dog trained to guide the blind, cannot tell a red light from a green one. When it leads its master across the street, it watches the traffic flow to tell when it is safe to cross.

THEY CALL IT PUPPY LOVE

According to a pet owner survey, 79 percent of Americans give their dogs holiday and/or birthday presents, and they dole out more cash for dog chow than baby food. Meanwhile, an American Animal Hospital Association poll showed that 33 percent of dog owners admit that they talk to their dogs on the phone or leave messages for them on an answering machine while away.

> More than 100,000 family dogs are killed each year in car accidents. As a result, a manufacturer in the eastern United States has developed a car restraint designed specifically for dogs riding in the car.
> Many early iron dog collars were studded with fearsome spikes. They were designed to protect hunting dogs' throats from attacks from the wolves, bears, and wild boar that roamed medieval European forests. Now collars inspired by the same design are found in novelty sex shops for humans.
> According to hospital figures, dogs bite an average of 1 million Americans a year. More people are killed in the United States each year by the jaws of dogs than have been killed by great white sharks in the last 100 years.

Course 241: **What's It Called?**

> A male goat that has been neutered is known as a *wether*.
> A male kangaroo is called a *boomer*, and a female is called a *flyer*.
> A pregnant goldfish is called a *twit*.
> The rear portion of the head of a horse is called the *poll*.

A whale's penis is called a *dork*. Know any dorks?

> A young male fur seal that is kept from the breeding grounds by the older males is called a *bachelor*. It might also be called frustrated!
> The belly scales on a snake are called *scutes*.
> The sound a camel makes is called *nuzzing*.

Course 222: **For the Birds**

> Bird droppings are a chief export of Nauru, an island nation in the western Pacific.
> Birds do not sing because they are happy. It is a territorial behavior.

During World War I, because of their acute hearing, parrots were kept on the Eiffel Tower to warn of approaching aircraft long before the planes were heard or seen by human spotters.

> The female pigeon cannot lay eggs if she is alone. In order for her ovaries to function, she must be able to see another pigeon. If no other pigeon is available, her own reflection in a mirror will suffice. Very narcissistic!
> Because birds carrying messages were often killed in flight by hawks, medieval Arabs made a habit of sending important messages twice. If they only had Fed-Ex.
> Flamingos are not naturally pink. They get their color from their food, tiny green algae that turn pink during digestion.

In zoos, ostriches are often unable to be sexually aroused unless they're being observed by human beings—which makes them total exhibitionists.

> Migrating geese fly in a V-formation to conserve energy. A goose's wings churn the air and leave an air current behind. In the flying wedge, each bird is in position to get a lift from the current left by the bird ahead. It is easier going for all, except the leader. During a migration, geese are apt to take turns in the lead position.

Ostriches are such fast runners, they can outrun a horse. Male ostriches can also roar like a lion.

> Owls have asymmetrical ears: one is directed downward, the other upward.
> Penguins have an organ above their eyes that converts seawater to freshwater.
> The Arctic tern holds the long-distance medal for travel, as he migrates from Antarctica to Massachusetts, logging up to 22,000 miles in stretches of up to 1,000 miles per week. Unfortunately, he does not rack up frequent flyer miles!
> The swan is the only bird that has a penis.

POLLY WANT A VALIUM?

Boredom can lead to madness in parrots. The birds need constant interaction, affection, and mental stimulation; bird authorities have determined that some parrots have the mental abilities of a 5-year-old human child. When caged by themselves and neglected for long periods of time, these intelligent, sociable birds can easily become mentally ill. Many inflict wounds upon themselves, develop strange tics, and rip out their own feathers. Should a neglected parrot go mad, there is little that can be done to restore it to normalcy. In England, there are mental institutions for such unfortunate creatures.

Seminar 1: **Animal Groups A–D**

A *shrewdness* of apes

A *troop* of baboons

A *shoal* of bass

A *sleuth* or *sloth* of bears

A *sounder* of boars

An *army* of caterpillars

A *clowder* or *clutter* of cats

A *brood* or *peep* of chickens

A *clutch* or *chattering* of chicks

A *quiver* of cobras

A *kine* of cows (twelve cows are a *flink*)

A *sedge* or *siege* of cranes

A *float* of crocodiles

A *murder* of crows

A *cowardice* of curs

A *dule* of doves

A *brace*, *paddling*, or *team* of ducks

Course 249: **Bats and Rats!**

> A baby bat is called a *pup*.
> A rat can fall from a 5-story building without injury.
> Vampire bats don't suck blood; they drink it. By making small cuts in the skin of a sleeping animal, the bat laps up the blood while its saliva numbs the area.

Don't worry about feeling drained. Vampire bats need only about two tablespoonfuls of blood each day. And the creature is able to extract its dinner in approximately 20 minutes.

> A rat can go without water longer than a camel can.
> A rat can squeeze through an opening no larger than a dime.

An anticoagulant from vampire bat saliva may soon be used to treat human heart patients.

> Contrary to popular misconception, bats do not become entangled in human hair and seldom transmit disease to other animals or humans.
> Rats can swim for a mile without resting, and they can tread water for 3 days straight.

Bad breath is likely to induce a bat to bite someone—so use that mouthwash today!

> Bat droppings in caves support whole ecosystems of unique organisms, including bacteria useful in detoxifying wastes, improving detergents, and producing gasohol and antibiotics.
> A mated pair of rats can produce up to 15,000 babies in one year.

Plants that are dependent on bats for pollination include bananas, dates, figs, cashews, avocados, saguaros, organ pipes, century plants, cloves, mangoes, breadfruit, carob, kapok, and almost every tropical night-blooming species, including the mescal plant. That's right—without bats, there would be no tequila!

HANGING OUT TOGETHER

Since bats are the only mammals who can fly, they failed to make great strides in the walking department. Their legs are not strong enough to support that function for long. For this reason, bats take the weight off their tired feet by hanging upside down. Their breast-feeding babes have no choice but to hang in limbo with Mom. Together, they reap the inverted benefits of downward gravitational pull.

Bats also invert our common beliefs regarding their eyesight. The bat, a nocturnal creature, hunts its prey at night, and rests up (or down, as is the case) for the evening's events by day. One would be incorrect in assuming that the bat has keen night vision, to assist it in its feeding frenzy. Not so. The bat employs an echo system, whereby it tosses out a high-frequency sound, inaudible to humans, which in turn strikes a target, and then bounces back to the bat, thereby letting it know what lies ahead. Were it not for the bat's radar, we would hear even more bumps in the night than we already do.

Course 232: **What a Pussy!**

> A cat keeps purring whether it is inhaling or exhaling—a baffling accomplishment.
> Cats with light-colored hair are six times less likely to trigger allergies in humans than those with black hair. Yet another reason to avoid a black cat crossing your path!
> Tests conducted by the University of Michigan concluded that while a dog's memory lasts no more than 5 minutes, a cat's can last as long as 16 hours—exceeding even that of monkeys and orangutans. No wonder your cat is still mad at you for kicking her off the bed last night.

Cats may copulate over 30 times a day. While a male feline may stalk a female for days at a time, once they mate, the entire sexual act only lasts a few seconds—not unlike certain humans!

> Despite its reputation for being finicky, the average cat consumes about 127,750 calories a year, nearly 28 times its own weight in food, and the same amount again in liquids. In case you were wondering, cats cannot survive on a vegetarian diet.

> Purring is heard in domesticated cats when they are petted, and in feral cats during sexual or other social contexts. Like a dog bearing her belly, purring may be a signal of appeasement to other cats or to people, a way to communicate that the purring cat is not threatened.

> A cat uses its whiskers to determine if a space is too small to squeeze through. The whiskers act as feelers or antennae, helping the animal to judge the precise width of any passage. And, because they aren't hampered by collarbones, cats can squeeze through any opening big enough to push their head through.

> A cat's jaw can't move sideways.

> When cats scratch furniture, it isn't an act of malice. They are actually tearing off the ragged edges of the sheaths of their claws to expose the new sharp ones beneath.

The possessor of a prize feline in Bucharest was able to increase her cat's stud fees to $1,000 a day—when its name was changed to Bill Clinton!

> Cats have amazing hearing ability. A cat's ear has 30 muscles that control the outer ear (by comparison, human ears only have 6 muscles). These muscles rotate 180 degrees, so the cat can hear in all directions without moving its head.

> Cats have more than one hundred vocal sounds, while dogs have only about 10.

> Lions, leopards, tigers, and jaguars are the only species of cats that can roar; but they can't purr.

> Cats, not dogs, are now the most common pets in America. Approximately 66 million cats to 58 million dogs are family pets, with parakeets flying a distant third at 14 million.

Although they were fearless in battle, Napoleon and Julius Caesar both suffered from *ailurophobia*, the severe fear of cats.

PHYSICS LESSON: THE LEGEND OF NINE LIVES

Surprisingly, a cat stands a greater chance of survival if it falls from a higher place than from a lower place. The laws of physics explain why: A falling object, after traveling a certain distance through the air, reaches a final speed, or "terminal velocity," because the object's friction with the air slows the fall. The smaller the object's mass, and the greater its area, the more it will slow.

A cat falling from a higher floor, after it stops accelerating, spreads its legs into an umbrella shape, which increases the area against which the air must push and increases the friction, thus slowing the cat's fall. A cat falling from a lower height does not have the opportunity to increase its body's area, slow its fall, or position his body to land on all four feet.

Seminar 2: Animal Groups E–L

A *gang* of elks

A *mob* of emus

A *business* or *fesnyng* of ferrets

A *charm* of finches

A *skulk* or *leash* of foxes

An *army* or *colony* of frogs

A *leash* of greyhounds

A *down* or *husk* of hares

A *cast* or *kettle* of hawks

A *brood* of hens

A *drift* or *parcel* of hogs

A *smack* of jellyfish

A *troop* or *mob* of kangaroos

An *ascension* or *exaltation* of larks

A *leap (leep)* of leopards

Course 289: That's a Croc!

> The crocodile cannot move his tongue. The whole tongue is rooted to the base of his mouth. So he can't stick out his tongue at you, but you can always stick your tongue out at him.
> A crocodile weighing only 120 pounds exerts a crushing force of about 1,540 pounds between its jaws. But no matter how much a human being weighs, his jaws still exert a puny force of only 40 to 80 pounds.

Crocodile eggs that are incubated below 85° Fahrenheit (29.5° Celsius) hatch into females, while those incubated above 95° Fahrenheit (35° Celsius) hatch into males.

> Within a lifetime, a crocodile can go through 2,000 to 3,000 teeth.
> The crocodile does not chew its food, but swallows it whole. It carries several pounds of small stones in its stomach to aid in grinding up and digesting its nourishment.

The crocodile is surprisingly fast on land. If pursued by a crocodile, a person should run in a zigzag motion, for the crocodile has little or no ability to make sudden changes of direction.

> Exhibiting cannibalistic tendencies, a crocodile will occasionally eat other crocodiles.
> The digestive juices of crocodiles contain so much hydrochloric acid that they have actually dissolved iron spearheads and 6-inch steel hooks they have swallowed. Yet crocs don't take Rolaids, as far as we know.

Sleeping with One Eye Open—**Literally!**

Marine mammals such as dolphins and whales manage to sleep without drowning, because only half their brain sleeps, while the other half stays awake and handles the breathing and swimming chores. The two hemispheres of their brains work totally independently. For 8 hours, the entire brain is awake. The left side then sleeps for 8 hours. When it wakes up, the right side sleeps for 8 hours. Thus, the marine mammals get 8 hours of sleep without ever having to stop physically.

Course 262: **Animal Relativity**

> Ten thousand insects are required to feed a single toad during the course of a typical summer.
> It takes 24 hours for a tiny newborn swan to peck its way out of its shell.
> An ostrich egg hatches in 42 days.

After 7 years, a lobster will grow to be 1 pound.

> It takes about 50 hours for a snake to digest one frog.
> A deep-sea clam can take up to 100 years to reach the length of three-tenths of an inch. The clam is among the slowest-growing, yet longest-living, species on earth.
> It takes an average of 18 hummingbirds to weigh in at 1 ounce.

Course 263: **Monkey Business**

> Male monkeys lose the hair on their heads in the same manner men do.
> A group of monkeys is called a *troop*.
> Hindus have a monkey for one of their gods. His name is Hanuman, and he is known for his mischievous sense of humor.

Scientific researchers say promiscuous species of monkeys appear to have stronger immune systems than less sexually active ones.

> The smallest monkey is the pygmy marmoset, which weighs around 5 ounces (150 grams). Baboons are the largest members of the monkey family.
> Gorillas do not know how to swim, and they sleep about 14 hours a day.
> Chimpanzees frequently engage in sex 20 or more times a day. Should there be no male around, the female of the species will take care of business by any means necessary.
> And just to prove how friendly they are, capuchin chimps occasionally welcome each other by displaying erections.

Something Stinks Down Under

It appears the sheep and cattle in Australia are farting up such a storm that all the released gas is aggravating the Greenhouse Effect. To help plug up the problem, and motivate ranch owners to take action, the government in Sydney has considered putting a tax on the critters' emissions.

The Useless Insect Institute

Roaches, mosquitoes, fleas, and other insects are among the most useless and annoying creatures—which is why they have their own academy here. While you may know that female mosquitoes are the ones who draw blood and spread disease, don't bother cursing at them—female mosquitoes are deaf. Also, it would pay to be prudent in the vicinity of the honeybee as it flits from flower to flower—not only because of its painful sting, but because each year the honeybee kills more people worldwide than venomous snakes.

By the way, be very thankful your HMO hasn't studied the medical practices of ancient India, or it might come up with some new kinds of coverage for you. At one time, Indian doctors used insect mandibles instead of stitches to bind the two sides of a cut together. The head of a large ant would be removed, and its pincers would be brought together through the patient's flesh. Isn't that disgusting? Well, that's nothing compared to what's lying ahead of you now!

Course 264: **Raid!**

> Biologists have discovered that cockroaches can change course as often as 25 times in one second, making them the most nimble animals known.

Close to 20 percent of all adults living in the United States have had a cockroach living in their inner ear canal. The roach enters the ear while you sleep.

> Cockroaches have quite a capacity for survival. If the head of one is removed carefully, so as to prevent it from bleeding to death, the cockroach can survive for several weeks. When it dies, it is from starvation.

Crushed cockroaches can be applied to a stinging wound to help relieve the pain.

> Cockroaches sample food before it enters their mouths and learn to shun foul-tasting poisons. They are opportunists and will eat wallpaper or TV cords. Cockroaches will even become cannibals if food is scarce.

Like Crunchy Foods?

Entomophagy is the scientific name for insect eating. There are more than 1,450 recorded species of edible insects. Many species of insects are lower in fat and higher in protein and have a better food-to-meat ratio than beef, lamb, pork, or chicken.

Course 265: **The Original Web Masters**

> Animals that have 3 pairs of legs such as insects, belong to the class *Insecta*. Animals with 4 pairs of legs belong to the class *Arachnida*.
> A spider is not an insect. It is an *arachnid*—it has 8 legs instead of 6, and has no wings or antennae. The same is true of the daddy longlegs, scorpion's mite, and tick—none is technically part of the insect class.

Australian scientists have identified some species of baby spiders that bite off the limbs of their mothers and slowly dine on them over a period of weeks. Researchers hypothesize that this maternal sacrifice keeps the young from eating one another.

> After mating, the female black widow spider turns on her partner and devours him. The female may dispatch as many as 25 suitors a day in this manner.
> Giant crab spiders have such a ferocious appearance that they earned a spot as extras in the horror film *Arachnophobia*. These creatures, however,

eat only cockroaches, crickets, and caterpillars, more than compensating for their scary appearance. Giant crab spiders are about 2 inches long, are hairy, and have noticeable black fangs and black feet. Their egg sac is the size of a golf ball.

Spiders never spin webs in structures made of chestnut wood. That is why so many European chateaux were built with chestnut beams—spider webs on a 50-foot beamed ceiling can be hard to remove.

> One ounce of the material that constitutes a spider's web could stretch 2,000 miles.
> While many arachnids rely on webs or trapdoors to catch prey, the bird-eating spider rushes straight at anything that moves. This hairy, venomous creature with a leg span that reaches 10 inches can eat grounded birds or small rodents.

JUST SAY NO!

Scientists at NASA tested the effects of certain human drugs on a spider's ability to spin webs. A spider on marijuana tried to make a web, but gave up when it was only half-done. Spiders on Benzedrine, or speed, spun webs quickly, but left huge holes in them, making odd patterns. Spiders on caffeine only spun some random threads, while those on sleeping pills never bothered to start making a web.

Course 266: The Buzz Around Town

> A bee has 5 eyes, 2 large compound eyes on either side of its head, and 3 *ocelli* (primitive eyes) on top of its head to detect light intensity.

Only female bees work. Males remain in the hive, their only mission in life being to fertilize the queen bee on her maiden flight. After they have served their function, the males are not allowed back into the hive but are left outside, where they starve to death.

> Honeybees navigate by using the Sun as a compass, even when it is hidden behind clouds—they find it via the polarization of ultraviolet light from areas of blue sky.
> The orchid releases a chemical that makes bees drunk. When the bee becomes disoriented, it dumps its load of pollen into the flower, thus pollinating the flower.

> A bumblebee uses 22 muscles to sting, but it does not die when it stings—it can sting again and again. In bumblebee hives, the entire colony, except for the queen, dies at the end of each summer.
> The intense fear of bees is called *apiphobia*.

Never squash a wasp that has stung you. Upon being crushed, it will release a chemical that becomes airborne; this signals guard wasps to come and sting whatever gets in their way.

Course 267: **Getting Antsy**

> The ant has the largest brain in the animal kingdom, in proportion to its size.
> An ant can lift 50 times its own weight, which is equivalent to a human being pulling a 10-ton trailer.
> Ants keep slaves. Certain species—the so-called sanguinary ants, for example—raid the nests of other ant tribes, kill the queen, and kidnap many of the workers. The workers are brought back to the captors' hive, where they are forced to perform menial tasks.

Ants stretch when they wake up. They also appear to yawn in a very human manner before taking up the tasks of the day.

> It is difficult to drown an ant because water doesn't penetrate their minuscule breathing tube; the ants will suffer, however, from too much carbon dioxide, which knocks them out. It takes awhile, but they will eventually die.
> Termite queens are fertilized regularly by the same mate for life, unlike bee and ant queens, whose male partners die after the first and only mating. They live up to 50 years.

THE DEMILITARIZED ZONE

Massed opposing armies fight each other along a front. The fighting continues for days, and millions die. This is not trench warfare among men. The armies are the weaver ants of African forests. The ants are so fierce that when the battle is resolved and the boundaries of the opposing colonies have been fixed, a "no-ant's-land" exists between them, where ants from each side do not dare to enter.

Course 268: **Don't Bug Me!**

> Only female mosquitoes drink blood. Male mosquitoes are vegetarians and do not bite, but feed on the nectar of flowers.

> Mosquitoes do not bite; they stab. A mosquito has no jaws; when attacking a victim, it pierces it with its long proboscis and sucks the blood up through a nasal tube.

Mosquito repellents don't repel; they hide you. The spray or lotion blocks the mosquito's sensors; however, it will seek out unprotected areas of skin.

> Mosquitoes are attracted to the color blue twice as much as to any other color.
> Mosquitoes have been responsible for more human deaths throughout history than all wars combined.
> The hardiest of all the world's insects is the mosquito. It has been found in the coldest regions of northern Canada and Siberia, and can live quite comfortably at the North Pole. It is equally at home in equatorial jungles.

In 1939, Pacific Grove, California, gained international attention by passing an ordinance making it a misdemeanor to molest a butterfly.

Course 269: **Beetle-Mania!**

> Fireflies are actually beetles.
> Iridescent beetle shells were the source of the earliest eye glitter ever used—devised by the ancient Egyptians.
> The Goliath beetle of Africa has a huge armor that makes it the heaviest flying insect in the world. In fact, it weighs more than eight mice and is a common pet with African children, who fly it from a string.

The Japanese beetle, found in the eastern United States and Canada, is the only bug in these countries you need be concerned about if it becomes lodged in your ear, for it can chew through your eardrum in a matter of minutes. Other bugs can be removed without the same urgency.

> There are more beetles on Earth than any other type of creature. Within the beetle family, the number of species alone is nearly a quarter-million.
> Usually bushmen hunt with poison arrows. The poison is extracted from the pupae of beetles found in the soil beneath infested marula trees. A few drops of the poison squeezed onto an arrow are enough to kill an antelope; one drop of it can kill a human if it enters his bloodstream.

Course 270: **Instant Insect Stats!**

> The caterpillar has more than 2,000 muscles.

> The common housefly is faster—in one sense—than a jet airplane. The fly moves 300 times its body length in one second, while the jet, at the speed of sound, travels 100 times its body length in one second.
> A grasshopper can leap over obstacles 500 times its own height. In relation to its size, it has the greatest jumping ability of all creatures.
> If humans could jump like fleas, they'd be able to leap over a 100-story building in a single bound.

If one places a tiny amount of liquor on a scorpion, it will instantly go mad and sting itself to death.

> Insects and arachnids make up 80 percent of all the animal species on Earth. There are over 5 million species of insects and arachnids in all.
> The weight of the world's insect population exceeds that of humankind by a factor of 12.
> Scientists discover approximately 7,000 to 10,000 new insect species every year—and it is believed that there are between 1 million and 10 million species yet unfound.
> The monarch butterfly can discern tastes 12,000 times more subtle than those perceivable by human taste buds.

Quick Cootie Quiz

1. According to the U.S. Department of Agriculture, the best time to spray household insects is 8:00 A.M., because insects are most vulnerable at this time.

True or False?

2. The Japanese have developed certain native plants that poison or repel insects within their homes, because bugs really bug them.

True or False?

3. Dragonflies aren't flies.

True or False?

4. The buzzing of flies and bees is not produced by any sound-producing apparatus within their bodies. It is simply the sound of their wings moving up and down at a rapid rate.

True or False?

5. There is really no such thing as cooties. It's just a nonsense word used by children to describe unpleasant insects.

True or False?

ANSWERS

1. FALSE. The best time is 4:00 P.M.

2. FALSE. Bugs hold a special place in the hearts of many Japanese, who often keep crickets, beetles, and fireflies as pets. Their calls are considered extremely soothing and remind the nature-loving Japanese of a simply, less hectic age.

3. TRUE.

4. TRUE

5. TRUE. However, most people believe that cooties are, in fact, a kind of body lice.

Course 271: Slinky and Kinky

> A group of rattlesnakes is called a *rhumba*.
> A snake has 2 penises, which may come in handy, since they mate for at least 24 hours at a time.
> A snake has no ears. However, its tongue is extremely sensitive to sound vibrations. By constantly flicking its tongue, the snake picks up these sound waves. In this sense, a snake "hears" with its tongue.
> There are some 50 different species of sea snakes, and all of them are venomous. They thrive in abundance along the coast from the Persian Gulf to Japan and around Australia and Melanesia. Their venom is 10 times as virulent as that of the cobra. Humans bitten by them have died within 24 hours.
> A snake is capable of eating an animal 4 times larger than the width of its own head. Most varieties of snake can go an entire year without eating a single morsel of food.

The gastric juices of a snake can digest bones and teeth—but not fur or hair.

> Snakes do not have eyelids, so even when they're asleep they cannot close their eyes. But they do have a protective layer of clear scales, called *brille*, over their eyes.
> The spitting cobra can spit venom out through tiny holes in his fangs. Aiming for his victim's eyes, this snake can spit up to 6 feet (2 meters) with a 19-inch (0.5 centimeter) spread. This venom can blind you!

The flying snake of Java and Malaysia is able to flatten itself out like a ribbon and sail like a glider from tree to tree.

- Breathing for most snakes is accomplished with one lung only. The left lung is either greatly reduced in size or missing completely.
- Snakes do not urinate. The secrete and excrete uric acid, which is a solid, chalky, usually white substance.
- The biggest snake in the world is the anaconda of South America. The largest anaconda ever was 27 feet (8.45 meters) long and more than 3 feet (1 meter) around, with a weight close to a quarter-ton.

Even after it's dead, a snake can still kill you with its venom.

- Rattlesnakes gather in groups to sleep through the winter. Sometimes up to 1,000 of them will coil up together to keep warm.
- The king cobra is the biggest of all poisonous snakes and can grow over 13 feet long. A bite from a king cobra can kill an elephant in 4 hours.

Trying to suck the venom out of a snakebite will probably make it—and your condition—worse. Just head to the closest hospital ASAP!

This Really Sucks!

The bite of a leech is painless due to its own anaesthetic. It will gorge itself up to five times its body weight and then just fall off its victim. The first medical use of leeches dates back approximately 2,500 years. The leech's saliva contains a property that acts as an anticoagulant for human blood.

Course 275: Animal Family Values

- The male fox will mate for life, and if the female dies, he remains single for the rest of his life. However, if the male dies, the female will hook up with a new mate.
- Gender roles are reversed in more than 300 species of pipefish and sea horses. Males not only receive eggs from females to fertilize them, they also hold them in a brood pouch until the young are born live.

Coyotes are extremely loyal to their mates. If one is caught in a trap, the other will bring small game for it to eat; it will soak itself in a river to allow its thirsty mate to chew on its damp fur for water. It has been documented that the free coyote will stay with its captive partner until death.

- During the mating season, competing male porcupines bristle their quills at each other and chatter their teeth in rage before attacking. All porcupines at this time become very vocal: grunting, whining, chattering, even barking and mewing at each other.

> Just like people, mother chimpanzees often develop lifelong relationships with their offspring. Are these called mama's chimps?

> It is the female lion who does more than 90 percent of the hunting, while the male is afraid to risk his life, or simply prefers to rest by watching TV.

The female knot-tying weaverbird will refuse to mate with a male who has built a shoddy nest. If spurned, the male must take the nest apart and completely rebuild it in order to win the affections of the female.

> Plains zebras establish harmonious harems. Harem masters have exclusive mating rights with up to 6 mares. Zebra harems are so stable that the mares remain associated with each other for life. Their foals have additional protection from the family stallion's readiness to defend his mates and offspring against all threats to their survival.

> The male sea lion may have more than 100 wives, which is more than many Mormons.

THE WORLD'S COLDEST PROFESSION

The female Adelie penguin, desperate to obtain the stones she uses to build her nest, visits the nest of a bachelor Adelie, goes through the entire courtship routine, and mates with him. But once the two have had sex, the female collects the stones she came for as a sort of payment, and waddles back home to her *actual* mate, who's been keeping the nest nice and warm for her return! She then stays with him for the rest of her life. Sometimes, especially cunning females engage in the courtship ritual, minus the mating part, grab the rocks, and dash home. Luckily, the males of this species, unlike humans, do not seem to bear a grudge.

The Most Shocking Animal

The electric eel has thousands of electric cells, with those organs making up four-fifths of its body. It lives in the Amazon River and its tributaries and is the most shocking animal on Earth—no other animal packs such a big charge. If attacking a large prey, a 9-foot-long eel can discharge about 800 volts. One zap could easily stun a human senseless. The larger the eel, the bigger the charge. The electric eel's shocking power is so great that it can overtake its victims while 15 feet away.

A telegram was sent to Eleanor Roosevelt from the 1939 World's Fair in New York using only the current from electric eels.

Course 276: **There's Something Fishy Here**

> A stingray never actually sees its food as it eats, since its eyes are on top of its head and its mouth and nostrils are on the bottom. This would certainly be an advantage at certain restaurants.

> A jellyfish is not a single animal but a colony of animals. Some tentacles act as a balance, others sting enemies, some catch prey, while others are in charge of breeding. Jellyfish are more than 95 percent water and have no brain, heart, or bones, and no actual eyes.

> A plaice, a large European flounder, can lie on a checkerboard and reproduce on its upper surface the same pattern of squares, for camouflage. But it still doesn't get invited to many parties.

A single piranha, with its razor-sharp teeth, is still dangerous enough when out of water to rip off the flesh—even a finger or toe—of an unwary fisherman.

> Goldfish lose their color if they are kept in a dim light or are placed in a body of running water, such as a stream. They remain gold when kept in a pond or in a bowl with adequate illumination.

> Fish scales are used to brighten eye shadow, nail polish, and lipstick. So if something's a little fishy about the gal you're kissing...

> A species of sponge called the red sponge can be pushed through a piece of fabric so that it is broken into thousands of tiny pieces. But the animal does not die. Rather, all the pieces reassemble until the sponge returns to its original form. Now, if only humans could do that when they go to pieces!

A 42-foot sperm whale has about 7 tons of oil in it, not sperm!

> Fish have been known to produce offspring with five heads on one body.

> The largest jellyfish in the world has a bell that can reach 8 feet across and tentacles that extend over half the length of a football field.

Most tropical marine fish could survive in a tank filled with human blood.

> The lungfish can live on dry land in a state of suspended animation for 3 years.

> Fish can survive the winter in polar regions without freezing. They owe their survival to chemicals in their blood that prevent it from freezing, much like antifreeze in a car.

> The gurnard, a fish found in Florida, grunts when a thunderstorm is brewing, and it's said to be more reliable than local meteorologists.

AM I BLUE?

A blue whale can grow as long as 3 Greyhound buses and heavier than 35 elephants. Its tongue alone is the size of a small car and weighs as much as an elephant. While immense, a blue whale's heart beats only nine times per minute. Yet blue whales can also produce extreme sounds of more than 185 decibels—nearly twice as loud as a jumbo jet at takeoff.

Seminar 3: **Animal Groups L–R**

A *pride* of lions

A *plague* of locusts

A *tiding* of magpies

A *stud* of mares

A *labour* of moles

A *barren* or *span* of mules

A *parliament* of owls

A *company* of parrots

A *covey* of partridges

A *muster* or *ostentation* of peacocks

A *nest, nide (nye)*, or *bouquet* of pheasants

A *string* of ponies

A *pod* of porpoises

A *covey* or *bevy* of quail

A *nest* of rabbits

An *unkindness* of ravens

Five Flipper Facts

1. A dolphin can remember a specific tone far better than a human can.

2. Dolphins have killed sharks by ramming them with their snouts.

3. A dolphin's hearing is so acute that it can detect underwater sounds from 15 miles away.

4. Dolphins jump out of the water to conserve energy. It is easier to move through the air than through the water.

5. In the water, dolphins have been known to approach human women and stroke their penises against them.

Between Two Worlds

Slime molds are half fungus and half bacteria. They live on the floor of South American rain forests and slither around like animals in search of food while, like a plant, they scatter spores that will become more slime molds.

Course 282: **Getting a Good Jump**

> Kangaroos usually give birth to one offspring annually. The young kangaroo, or *joey*, is only about an inch long—no bigger than a waterbug.
> A kangaroo mother holds a reserve embryo inside of her after her first baby has crawled into her pouch. This serves as an emergency back-up baby, should the first one die prematurely.
> A kangaroo cannot jump if its tail is lifted off the ground. It needs its tail for pushing off.

Tennis pro Evonne Goolagong's last name means "Kangaroo's Nose" in one of Australia's Aboriginal languages.

> In silent Aboriginal hunting language, a closed hand slowly opening is meant to show that a kangaroo is near.
> Kangaroos can move as fast as 30 miles per hour and can leap up to 25 feet in the air.
> The typical kangaroo is 40 percent brighter than the smartest dog or cat.
> A group of kangaroos is called a *mob*.

Course 284: **One Hump or Two?**

> The humps on a camel's back are not water. They are actually huge heaps of fat and flesh that can weigh as much as 80 pounds in a healthy camel. But the backbone of a camel is straight, not curved.
> Camels eat just about anything. When camels are really hungry and there is no food around, they won't think twice about gobbling up people's tents, sandals, or blankets.

A giraffe can go without water longer than a camel can.

> A camel can lose up to 30 percent of its body weight in perspiration and continue to cross the desert. A human would die of heat shock after sweating away only 12 percent of his body weight.
> Camels have 3 eyelids to protect themselves from blowing sand, and a camel can shut its nostrils during a desert sandstorm.
> A camel with one hump is called a *dromedary*; a camel with two humps is a *Bactrian*.

The hump of a starving camel may flop over and hang down the side of its body as the fat is used up.

> Camel milk is the only milk that doesn't curdle when boiled.

> In Morocco, camel races are a popular sport, since camels can run as fast as horses. Camel fighting also attracts audiences in several countries around the world—so these humps can obviously take their lumps!

Course 285: **Working for Peanuts**

> Elephants sleep only 2 hours a day and can remain standing after they die.
> Elephant herds post their own sentries. Whenever danger threatens, the lookout raises its trunk, and though it may be as far as a half-mile away, the rest of the herd is instantly alerted. How this communication takes place is not understood.
> In old Siam (today's Thailand), white elephants were so rare that they were automatically the property of the emperor. To punish people, the emperor would give them a white elephant, because while they had to care for it, they were forbidden to ride or work it. Hence, the modern term for something totally useless: *a white elephant*.

Genuine ivory does not only come from elephants. It can come from the tusks of a boar or a walrus.

> Elephants communicate in sound waves below the frequencies that humans can hear.
> There are 40,000 muscles and tendons in an elephant's trunk. This makes it very strong and flexible, allowing an elephant to pluck a delicate flower, untie a knot, or tear a tree out of the ground; yet the trunk is sensitive enough to smell water 3 miles away.
> Until he's about 21 years old, the male Indian elephant isn't interested in romancing a female elephant.

The average elephant produces 50 pounds of dung each day.

Seminar 4: **Animal Groups S–Z**

A *dray* of squirrels

A *murmuration* of starlings

A *mustering* of storks

A *flight* of swallows

A *bevy, herd, lamentation, or wedge* of swans

A *sounder* or *drift* of swine

A *hover* of trout

A *rafter* of turkeys

A *bale* of turtles

A *pitying* or *dule* of turtledoves

A *pod* of walrus

A *fall* of woodcocks

A *descent* of woodpeckers

Course 291: **The Fastest!**

> The fastest animal on four legs is the cheetah, which races at speeds up to 70 miles per hour in short distances. It can accelerate to 45 miles per hour in two seconds.
> The greyhound, the fastest dog, can reach speeds of up to 45 miles per hour. The breed was known to exist in ancient Egypt more than 5,000 years ago.

THE FIVE FASTEST BIRDS ARE

1. the peregrine falcon—175 mph

2. the spine-tailed swift—106 mph

3. the frigate bird—95 mph

4. the spur-winged goose—88 mph

5. the red-breasted merganser—80 mph

> Beneath the sea, the fastest of all fish is the swordfish, streaming forward at speeds near 68 miles per hour.
> Bears can easily overtake even the fastest Olympic sprinter.
> A two-day-old gazelle can outrun a full-grown horse.

Course 298: **Shark Attack**

> Sharks and rays are the only animals known to man that cannot succumb to cancer. Scientists believe this is related to the fact that they have no bone—only cartilage. They also don't smoke.
> Sharks can detect bright or high-contrast clothing a lot more easily than dull or matching clothing, so it might be wise to dress accordingly no matter what the fashion trend might be. Leave that jewelry at home for the same reason.
> While some sharks lay eggs, blue sharks give birth to live pups, as do about two-thirds of all sharks, estimated at nearly 350 species.

Sharks can be dangerous even before they are born. One scientist was bitten by a sand tiger shark embryo while he was examining its pregnant mother.

> The embryos of tiger sharks fight each other while in their mother's womb, the survivor being the baby shark that is born. Talk about sibling rivalry!
> Shark fossil records date back more than twice as far as those of the dinosaurs.
> Sharks have a sixth sense that enables them to detect bioelectrical fields radiated by other sea creatures and to navigate by sensing changes in the earth's magnetic field.

> Some sharks swim in a figure eight when frightened.
> The biggest fish in the world are the whale shark at 50,000 pounds, the basking shark at 32,000 pounds, the great white shark at 7,000 pounds, the Greenland shark at 2,250 pounds, and the tiger shark at 2,070 pounds.

The mechanical shark in the 1975 hit movie *Jaws* was named Bruce.

Final Exam

1. Scientists say that pigs, unlike all other domestic animals, arrive at solutions by thinking them through.

True or False?

2. The albatross can glide on air currents for several days and can even have sex while in flight.

True or False?

3. A chicken will lay bigger eggs with thicker shells if the lighting is changed in such a way as to make them think a day is 28 hours long.

True or False?

4. A cow can give milk even if she hasn't given birth to a calf.

True or False?

5. A hippopotamus's scream during sex has been recorded at 115 decibels—louder than a jet at takeoff.

True or False?

6. When baby giraffes are born, their mothers immediately place them gently on a pile of gathered leaves.

True or False?

7. Frogs drink in water by expanding their necks and then sucking it in through their nose.

True or False?

8. Hippopotamuses have killed more people in Africa than all the lions, elephants, and water buffalo combined.

True or False?

9. You can lead a cow downstairs, but not upstairs.

True or False?

10. The only country in the world that has a Bill of Rights for Cows is Pakistan.

True or False?

ANSWERS

1. TRUE.

2. FALSE. They can sleep in flight;

3. TRUE.

4. FALSE: A cow can't give milk until she's given birth to a calf.

5. TRUE.

6. FALSE. The mothers drop them six feet to the ground, and they land on their heads.

7. FALSE: Frogs never drink. They absorb water from their surroundings by osmosis.

8. TRUE: They kill people by trampling them.

9. FALSE: Just the reverse is true.

10. FALSE: But the answer is close; it's India.

3

The USELESS
School of
Television

Doctors in Sri Lanka all agree: immense portions of the human brain are devoted to storing decades of television information, which in turn is crowding out other pertinent facts like the name of your son's orthodontist or your spouse's lawyer. Studies have also concluded that data about TV personalities are extremely bulky, with a massive 30 gigabytes of space on the hard drive of your mind given over to Bryan Gumbel alone, leaving just 3 bytes to recall where you left your car keys—or even where you left your car.

Nevertheless, Useless TV Replacement Therapy will revitalize your dormant gray matter with facts like: on TV's *Dragnet*, Sergeant Joe Friday's badge number was 714. But even more amazingly, the number 714 appears mysteriously again—714 Evergreen Terrace, Springfield, is the address of *The Simpsons*. Plus, in a totally unrelated item regarding numbers, TV's Judge Judy Sheindlin is a petite size 2, and her silk judge robe cost $400.

Which is the great thing about USELESS KNOWLEDGE—it doesn't have to be rational. It doesn't have to make sense. You just spurt it out. Nothing could be simpler. You might ask folks what the sitcoms *Everybody Loves Raymond* and *Frasier* have in common. Well, Ray's brother is a police officer, and Frasier's father is a retired cop. And speaking of the police, band leader Andy Summers of HBO's *The Dennis Miller Show* used to play with what rock band? You got it—the Police!

Whether your favorite show is *The West Wing* or *Jeopardy*, turn off the TV set right now—because this is the kind of information you won't get even by watching Dan Rather.

Course 1001: Before They Got with the Program

> Before starring on *Bonanza* or *Little House on the Prairie*, Michael Landon worked as an operator for a machine that sealed hot cans of Campbell's Tomato Soup.
> Former president Ronald Reagan served as host of television's *Death Valley Days*.

When she was a young woman, TV sex therapist Dr. Ruth Westheimer lived in Israel. There, she was a trained sniper. In fact, she was so adept at handling a Sten gun—a British submachine gun—that she could quickly assemble one while blindfolded.

> Former *Good Morning, America* cohost Joan Lunden's birth name was Joan Blunden.
> Former *Saturday Night Live* cast member Chevy Chase's real first name is Cornelius, and comedian Rodney Dangerfield's real name is Jacob Cohen.

> Bob Newhart graduated with a B.S. degree in commerce from Loyola University, and worked as an accountant before he tried his hand at comedy.

Some animal-related jobs held by entertainers before they achieved fame and fortune include birdcage cleaner (Desi Arnaz), shepherd (Raymond Burr), and fishing boat unloader (Kelsey Grammer).

> Peter Falk, best known for his starring role on TV's *Columbo*, earned a B.S. in political science from the New School for Social Research in New York. He worked as an efficiency expert for the Connecticut budget director before he pursued acting.
> Fred Rogers, the creator and star of the award-winning children's program *Mr. Rogers' Neighborhood*, is an ordained Presbyterian minister.
> Before his success in *Dobie Gillis* and *Gilligan's Island*, Bob Denver had been a schoolteacher.

When actor Michael J. Fox first auditioned for the TV series *Family Ties,* he was $35,000 in debt and living on macaroni and cheese.

> Phil Donahue earned a B.A. in theology from the University of Notre Dame before becoming a renowned talk-show host.
> Before landing a small recurring TV role on CBS's *Murphy Brown* and then a regular supporting role as British physical therapist Daphne Moon on NBC's *Frasier*, Jane Leeves was a fingernail-accessory package stuffer.

Pee-Wee Herman was a Fuller Brush salesman.

> Before he became a home-repair guru on U.S. television, Bob Vila was a Peace Corps volunteer in Panama.
> Julia Child worked as an advertising copywriter for a furniture store before she became the "queen of cuisine" and darling of TV's PBS.

During World War II, before James Arness portrayed U.S. marshall Matt Dillon in *Gunsmoke*, he was the first American soldier to jump off his boat at the Anzio beachhead. He was ordered to do so by his commanding officer because, standing at 6'8", Arness was the tallest man in his company, and the water's depth needed to be tested as a safety precaution.

> Before Britney Spears, Christina Aguilera, Justin Timberlake, J. C. Chasez of *'N Sync*, and Keri Russell of TV's *Felicity* went on to fame and fortune, they appeared on the revamped *Mickey Mouse Club* on the Disney Channel.
> Goldie Hawn was a dancer until she was spotted in the chorus line of a 1966 Andy Griffith special. Her first acting role was as a gossipy neighbor in the

one-season comedy series *Good Morning, World* in 1967. From there, Hawn went on to *Rowan and Martin's Laugh-In* and stardom.

> Before his debut on *Magnum, P.I.*, Tom Selleck appeared twice on *The Dating Game*, but didn't get picked either time.
> Oprah Winfrey was Miss Fire Prevention before becoming queen of the talk shows.

Before *Dallas* went on the air, the working title of the TV series was *Houston*.

WIND IN THEIR SALES

Before they hit it big in show business, Carol Burnett sold handbags in a shoe store, Ellen DeGeneres sold vacuum cleaners, David Hyde Pierce sold clothing, Jerry Seinfeld sold lightbulbs, and Jerry Van Dyke sold Bibles. One of the icons of stand-up comedy, Rodney Dangerfield, sold aluminum siding to put food on the table.

Course 1013: Mad-vertising

> In the late 1970s, the Coca-Cola Company boycotted the NBC late-night comedy show *Saturday Night Live* for several years. The giant soda company was retaliating against a frequent character of comedian John Belushi—a Greek restaurant owner who repeatedly said to customers, "No Coke—Pepsi," thus saying the rival company's name dozens of times within each skit.
> There are two more victims of the Coke and Pepsi war. Joan Crawford and Bette Davis had been feuding for years. During the making of *Whatever Happened to Baby Jane?*, Davis had a Coca-Cola machine installed on the set due to Crawford's affiliation with Pepsi—she was the widow of Pepsi's CEO. Crawford exacted her revenge by putting weights in her pockets when Davis had to drag her across the floor during certain scenes.

Got paint thinner? In most TV milk commercials, a mixture of white paint with a little thinner is used instead of milk.

> When he was introduced in TV ads in October 1965, the Pillsbury Doughboy became instantly popular with women consumers. Poppy's signature belly poke and giggle have become synonymous with the Pillsbury company.
> The voice of the animated Colonel Sanders in Kentucky Fried Chicken commercials in the late 1990s was supplied by Randy Quaid.
> Among the celebrities seen in Japanese ads have been noodle pitchman Arnold Schwarzenegger and whiskey endorser Steven Spielberg.

> It was reported in January 2000 that ostrich producers were attempting to lure CBS personality David Letterman to become a spokesman for their product. They said that less-fatty ostrich meat made into "ostrich and tortellini soup" was perfect for someone like Letterman, who was then recovering from quintuple-bypass heart surgery.

Since pop star Britney Spears signed on for its TV commercials in 2000, I-Zone has become the number-one-selling camera in the United States.

> In 1982, young Sarah Michelle Gellar acted in the first commercial ever to mention a competitor by name. For Burger King, she claimed that the burgers of Burger King's competitor were "smaller." McDonald's sued her as well as Burger King. In the same commercial she claimed, "I only eat at Burger King." After that, Gellar couldn't eat at a McDonald's unless she was in disguise.
> At age 11, long before her leap to international fame in the blockbuster film *Titanic*, Kate Winslet costarred with a creature called Honey Monster in a British TV commercial for a breakfast cereal.

A TV commercial for what personal product uses the Rod Stewart song "Forever Young"? Pampers!

RESIDUAL FAME

Comedian Bill Cosby became the spokesperson for Jell-O pudding in 1974. His upbeat, childlike personality worked well with on-screen youngsters, and he later began the "Kids Love Pudding" TV campaign. By the late 1980s and early 1990s, Cosby became the uncontested king of product endorsements. By 1992, he was earning approximately $125,000 an hour, or $1 million a day, and he is still going strong today.

Two News-unworthy Items

1. For many years, the globe on *NBC Nightly News* spun in the wrong direction. On January 2, 1984, NBC finally set the world spinning back in the proper direction.

2. In June 1995, as KVEW-TV reporter Mychal Limric was doing a news story on beekeeping in Kennewick, Washington, the bees took an apparent liking, or disliking, to his hair gel, said the station's news director. The bees attacked him from a hive 50 feet away. Limric was treated for more than 30 stings on the scalp and face. He was the only person there who was stung.

Course 1032: **Where No One Has Gone...**

> Captain Kirk's *Enterprise* crew numbered 430. His successor, Captain Picard, had 1,012 under his command.

> Before she was cast as the sultry Uhura on the 1960s *Star Trek*, Nichelle Nichols performed as a singer with Duke Ellington.

> The name of the USS *Enterprise* in the original draft for the *Star Trek* TV series was the USS *Yorktowne*.

> In the classic *Star Trek* series, Doctor McCoy's nickname was Bones, but his little-used first name was Leonard.

William Shatner and Nichelle Nichols, as Capt. James T. Kirk and Communications Officer Lt. Uhura, shared network television's first interracial kiss in the *Star Trek* episode "Plato's Children." The revolutionary segment aired in 1968.

> At the age of 8, Leonard Nimoy (Mr. Spock) began performing in a local community theater in Boston. Later, when he moved to Los Angeles, he joined a Yiddish theater group.

> Leonard Nimoy directed the films *Three Men and a Baby* and *The Good Mother* with Diane Keaton as well as *Star Trek IV: The Voyage Home*.

> Which *Star Trek* captain starred as Captain Ahab in a TV remake of *Moby Dick*? Patrick Stewart, of course!

> *Star Trek* fans in over 120 countries lament the fact that Patrick Stewart has never won an Emmy Award for his role as Capt. Jean-Luc Picard on *Star Trek: The Next Generation*.

What Iowa city is the future birthplace of *Star Trek*'s Captain Kirk? Riverside!

> The 1997–98 season of *Star Trek: Voyager* saw the introduction of a sexy new female character: Seven of Nine—a member of the Borg collective who got unplugged from her dronelike comrades.

> The *Star Trek: The Next Generation* series introduced the ultracapitalistic and ultrashort alien race called the Ferengi.

> Reportedly, in December 1995 British researchers discovered that at least 10 percent of the zealous *Star Trek* fans they queried had unstable personalities and took the science-fiction franchise too seriously.

The name of the first space shuttle was the *Constitution*. Pres. Gerald Ford changed it to *Enterprise* after receiving 100,000 letters from *Star Trek* fans.

Course 1041: **Behind the Comedy Scenes**

> After 11 years of living together, Danny DeVito and Rhea Perlman were married during a *Taxi*-lunch break.
> One alternate title that had been considered, but then discarded, for NBC's hit *Friends* was *Insomnia Cafe*.
> Helen Hunt, award-winning costar of the TV sitcom *Mad About You* and the film *As Good As It Gets*, appeared on *The Mary Tyler Moore Show* when she was 7 years old as the daughter of Murray Slaughter.
> Long before *The Tonight Show*, Jay Leno was a regular cast member on the 1977 TV variety program *The Marilyn McCoo and Billy Davis, Jr. Show*, which so many of us recall fondly today.
> Johnny Carson delivered 4,531 opening monologues during his 30 years as host of *The Tonight Show*.

Johnny Carson would like his epitaph to read "I'll be right back."

> On the TV sitcom *The Addams Family*, it took actress Carolyn Jones 2 hours every day to put on Morticia's vampirish makeup. She also wore a full-length wig made of black human hair.
> Diminutive actor Felix Silla played the hirsute role of Cousin Itt on *The Addams Family*. Years later, he was Twiki on television's *Buck Rogers in the 25th Century* and also was one of the Ewoks in *Return of the Jedi*.

Gilda Radner was the first cast member hired for the original *Saturday Night Live* troupe; John Belushi was the last hired.

> In the *Mork and Mindy* series, the capital city of Mork's home planet, Ork, was Kork.
> The full name of Rhea Perlman's award-winning character on TV's *Cheers* was Carla Maria Victoria Angelina Teresa Apollonia Lozupone Tortelli LeBec.
> In 1959, Larry Linville, who played Maj. Frank Burns on TV's *M*A*S*H*, competed for and received a scholarship to the Royal Academy of Dramatic Arts in London.

Despite his tremendous popularity, Jackie Gleason never won an Emmy Award. But his sidekick, Art Carney, won five Supporting Actor Emmys for both *The Jackie Gleason Show* and *The Honeymooners*. Reportedly, this irked good friend Carney, who hid his trophies so that Gleason wouldn't be reminded of the industry snub when he visited Carney at his home.

> Jackie Gleason shares ranks with TV performers Andy Griffith, Bob Hope, Angela Lansbury, Bob Newhart, Cybill Shepherd, the Smothers Brothers,

Tim Allen, Hal Linden, and Jerry Seinfeld, none of whom have won Best Actor Emmys.

> Some viewers of *Gilligan's Island* apparently took the show seriously in the 1960s. The U.S. Coast Guard received several telegrams from concerned citizens asking why they didn't rescue the *Minnow*'s crew.
> The character of the Professor on *Gilligan's Island* was named Roy Hinkley. The Skipper was named Jonas Grumby. Both names were used only once in the entire series, on the first episode.
> On the hit *The Drew Carey Show*, the tongue-in-cheek name of one of Drew's best friends is Oswald Lee Harvey. (Lee Harvey Oswald assassinated Pres. John F. Kennedy. So is this funny?)

In every single episode of TV's *Seinfeld*, there is a Superman somewhere in at least one scene.

Course 1056: **Television Firsts**

> Philco Predicta was the name of the first TV set.
> Ellen DeGeneres was the first stand-up comedienne Johnny Carson ever asked to sit down on *The Tonight Show* guest couch during a first appearance.

The first television sitcom couple ever to share the same bed on a regular basis was gruesome twosome Lily and Herman Munster.

> Steve Allen was the first host of *The Tonight Show*, and Dave Garroway was the first host of *The Today Show*.
> The first TV soap opera, *Faraway Hill*, debuted on the DuMont network in 1946.

The first toilet ever seen on TV was on the comedy series *Leave It to Beaver*.

> The first toy product ever advertised on television was Mr. Potato Head®. Introduced in 1952, Mr. Potato Head took advantage of TV's explosive growth to gain access to tens of millions of newly plugged-in households.
> Bill Cosby became the first black leading actor in a TV drama series when he starred opposite Robert Culp on *I Spy*. He won 3 Best Actor in a Drama Series Emmys for his role as Alexander "Scotty" Scott.
> The first color TV series starred married actors Hume Cronyn and Jessica Tandy and was called *The Marriage*, appropriately enough.

On the forever-running *Wheel of Fortune*, who was the very first host? Not Pat Sajak, but Chuck Woolery.

> The first video featured on MTV was by the group the Buggles, and it was called *Video Killed the Radio Star*.
> Playtex made U.S. history in May 1987 when TV networks began airing its commercials showing women wearing bras. Prior to this, either torso mannequins were used, or female models donned brassieres on top of their outer clothing.
> The 1947 World Series brought in television's first mass audience. It was carried in New York, Philadelphia, Schenectady, and Washington, D.C., and was seen by an estimated 3.9 million people—with 3.5 million of them watching in pubs and bars.

The name of the first person to win the million-dollar prize on *Who Wants To Be a Millionaire?* was John Carpenter.

> George Carlin was the first host of *Saturday Night Live*, and Janis Ian was his first musical guest.
> *CBS Evening News*, with anchor Walter Cronkite, was network TV's first 30-minute evening newscast. It was expanded from its previous 15-minute format beginning with the September 3, 1963, telecast. At the end of that inaugural 30-minute show, Cronkite first uttered his famous tag line, "And that's the way it is."
> The first TV show ever to be put into reruns was *The Lone Ranger*.

The first American TV show to be seen in the People's Republic of China was *Baywatch*.

> The first Japanese-produced TV series to be exported to the U.S.A. was *Astro Boy*.
> In 1954, the first nationally televised Miss America Pageant was broadcast live to an audience of 27 million TV viewers.

The lavish coronation of Queen Elizabeth II was the first major international TV broadcast.

> *Captain Kangaroo*, starring Bob Keeshan, was the first TV network kids' show in the United States. CBS launched it in 1954.
> The first TV show ever to be watched by over 50 million households was the final episode of *M*A*S*H*.

Leonardo DiCaprio's first TV appearance was on *Romper Room*.

Course 1077: **Just a Little Offensive**

> *The Muppet Show* was banned from TV in Saudi Arabia because one of its
> stars was a pig.
> *The Untouchables*, which debuted in 1959 and starred Robert Stack, was the
> most violent television show of its time. It became the target of more protests
> from viewers than any other regular TV series to date. The show was even
> boycotted by mobsters over alleged unfair treatment.
> In 1999, the National Ethnic Coalition of Organizations organized a boycott
> of the Mafia-themed show *The Sopranos*, saying it presented a distorted
> view of the typical Italian-American family, and calling it "a horribly negative
> stereotype, an embarrassment and a slap in the face to every Italian-
> American in this country."

**In June 1994, the sitcom *Roseanne* was condemned by the
Media Research Center, a conservative media watchdog, as the
most biased and liberal show on TV.**

> A coalition of the fire-prevention groups demanded that Jim Carrey's Fire
> Marshall Bill comedy sketches on the program *In Living Color* be taken off the
> air because of the negative effect they were reportedly having on children.
> In March 1996, Pizza Hut and Taco Bell cancelled their $5.4 million sponsor-
> ship of ABC's new *The Dana Carvey Show* after some of Carvey's humor
> "went too far." One sketch that offended the sponsors featured a dancing
> taco that kept telling Carvey that he was a "whore" for pushing the sale of
> Pepsi products.
> Comedian/actor Billy Crystal portrayed Jodie Dallas, the first openly gay
> main character on network television, on ABC's *Soap*, which aired from
> 1977 to 1981. Various church groups protested the seeming "acceptance"
> of homosexuality.

**In October 1994, Amtrak railways cancelled $2 million in
advertising with The Tonight Show with Jay Leno to retaliate
against the frequent jokes Leno told on the show about the
railway. Amtrak had complained several times, demanding
that the wisecracks be stopped. Leno continued to take pot
shots, prompting Amtrak's cancellation.**

NOT FUNNY TIMES FOUR

1. In a tragic fall on *The Andy Williams Show* in 1965, comedian Jerry Lewis suffered a skull fracture that led to an addiction to the painkiller Percodan. His surprise reunion with former partner Dean Martin on the 1976 Muscular Dystrophy telethon made entertainment history, but Lewis said he was in such a drug fog, he didn't recall it and had to watch it on video.

2. After the attempted assassination of Ronald Reagan in the 1980s, William Katt's character name on TV's *The Greatest American Hero* was changed from Ralph Hinkley to Ralph Hanley to avoid any association with would-be assassin John Hinkley, Jr.

3. In October 1993, *Beavis and Butt-head*, MTV's animated top-rated series, was attacked for allegedly inspiring a 5-year-old child to start a fatal fire. In response, MTV agreed to run the controversial show in a later time spot, and the writers agreed that in the future they would not use references to fires.

4. Andy Kaufman, best known for his comedy work as Latka Gravas on the TV sitcom *Taxi*, died of lung cancer. Ironically, he was a lifelong nonsmoker.

Course 1087: *I Love Lucy*—the Untold Story

> Television's *I Love Lucy* began as a radio show, *My Favorite Husband*, in which Lucy played the scheming wife of a bank vice president. CBS wanted to move the show to television—but almost scrapped the idea because of Lucy's insistence that Desi Arnaz play her husband. Lucy persisted and finally got her way—the rest is TV history.

> Demand was great for *I Love Lucy* merchandise in the late 1950s. A Little Ricky doll debuted in stores, and its manufacturer couldn't keep up with the thousands of reorders. Neither could an overworked furniture firm that sold an unprecedented 1 million *I Love Lucy* bedroom suites to the show's fans in just 90 days.

> Legendary actress Bette Davis was Lucille Ball's classmate at John Murray Anderson's Dramatic School.

Lucille Ball was tossed out of drama school in New York when she was only 15 years old. The reason? Her instructors claimed that the future madcap comedienne was too quiet and shy.

> Television comedy queen Lucille Ball appeared on a record 29 covers of *TV Guide* magazine.

> Desi Arnaz, Jr., was on the cover of the first *TV Guide*.

DESI WAS A DOOZY!

Desi Arnaz's father was mayor of Santiago, Cuba, and his mother was the daughter of one of the founders of Bacardi Rum. His family went into exile in the United States after the coup that brought dictator Fulgencio Batista to power in 1934. The family made its new home in Miami, Florida. And Desi's best friend in high school? Al Capone, Jr.

Desi's heavy Cuban accent often made retakes necessary. His enunciation of "recognized talent" came out as "recognize Stalin." He said "ever thin" for "everything" and "mushing peectures" for "motion pictures," while "won't" was "wunt" and "Fred Mertz" was "Frat Mers."

Arnaz saw a dubbed *Lucy* show while in Japan and heard himself "speaking" Japanese. "It sounded so genuine," he later recalled, "that I had to ask how they handled my lousy English. 'It was easy,' said the producer. 'We just hired an actor who spoke lousy Japanese.'"

Course 1079: **Replacement Parts**

> Mickey Rooney turned down the role of Archie Bunker in the 1970s sitsom *All in the* Family. The former child star was convinced that the show would bomb, and he wasn't willing to jeopardize his professional reputation, although his film career had been on the skids for years. Little-known character actor Carroll O'Connor won the role as a result.

> Lisa Kudrow was originally cast as producer Roz on NBC's *Frasier*, but was fired and replaced before landing the role of ditzy free spirit Phoebe on NBC's *Friends*.

In the early 1970s, Gavin MacLeod initially read for the part of boss Lou Grant in the new TV sitcom *The Mary Tyler Moore Show*. MacLeod had played heavies and villains for years, and was a strong contender for the part of the gruff supervisor. After auditioning, he left, but then returned, asking to read for the role of sentimental Murray Slaughter. He got the part.

> Jack Lord wasn't the first choice for the role of Steve McGarrett on TV's *Hawaii Five-O*—Gregory Peck was.

> Bob Denver wasn't even in the running for the lead part on TV's *Gilligan's Island*. Jerry Van Dyke was the original choice, but he turned it down. Ultimately, Denver became Gilligan, and the show ran for three seasons. Twenty-five years after its last episode was filmed, it is still one of the most widely syndicated TV shows in television history.

> For the role of Mike Brady, the father on TV's *The Brady Bunch* in the 1970s, Robert Reed was ultimately selected. However, a strong contender for the patriarchal part was actor Gene Hackman.

Ingenue actress Neve Campbell once auditioned for TV's *Baywatch*. The casting director turned her down because he thought she was too pale.

> Gene Barry was the first choice for the role of accused murderer Dr. Richard Kimble in the 1960s TV drama *The Fugitive*, but turned it down. He later starred in *Burke's Law*, which ran from 1963 to 1966 and was revived in 1993. David Janssen was selected to play Dr. Kimble, and *The Fugitive* ran for four strong seasons.

Raised from the Dead

Michelle Pfeiffer, Susan Dey, Louis Gossett, Jr., Claude Akins, and David Hasselhoff have one lamentable thing in common: they were the lead cast members for ill-fated TV shows that were cancelled within a scant month's time. Pfeiffer was in *B.A.D. Cats* in 1980; Dey was in *Loves Me, Loves Me Not* in 1977; Gossett starred in *The Lazarus Syndrome* in 1980; Akins was in *Nashville 99* in 1977; and Hasselhoff, long before *Baywatch*, was in *Semi-Tough* in 1980.

Course 1089: **Cartoon Alley**

> Before she met Popeye, Olive Oyl went out with Ham Gravy.
> Although Superman was depicted as fighting for truth, justice, and the American way, he was cocreated by a Canadian. Toronto-born Joe Shuster created the Man of Steel in the 1930s with his friend Jerry Siegal.
> In 1949, *Crusader Rabbit* debuted as the first made-for-TV animated cartoon.

Film legend James Cagney narrated the first Smokey the Bear cartoon.

> TV's popular cartoon duo Rocky and Bullwinkle represented a number of General Mills cereals from 1959 to 1970: Cheerios, Cocoa Puffs, Jets, and Trix.
> The dapper Michigan J. Frog was created by master cartoonist Chuck Jones in the 1950s for a Warner Bros. cartoon, and now is the mascot of the Warner Bros. television network.

The extra month on the school calenders on *The Simpsons* was called Smarch.

> Betty Boop came into existence on August 9, 1930. She was supposed to be the girlfriend of Bimbo the dog, as competition for Disney's Mickey Mouse, and both characters were originally dogs with human characteristics. However, Bimbo was forgotten in the wake of Betty's growing popularity.
> The names of Popeye's four nephews are Pipeye, Peepeye, Pupeye, and Poopeye.

UH, WHAT'S UP, DOC?

Mel Blanc—the voice of Bugs Bunny—was actually allergic to carrots! After a near-fatal auto accident in 1961, Blanc did all of his cartoon work, including the first 60 episodes of *The Flintstones*, flat on his back, with the microphone hanging over his bed.

Course 1092: Are You Game?

> On TV game shows, a contestant who freezes before the camera is called a *Bambi*, in reference to a deer paralyzed by the glare of headlights.
> Bob Eubanks was a concert promoter before becoming the host of *The Newlywed Game* in 1966. In 1964, he brought the Beatles to the Hollywood Bowl.
> Regis Philbin's childhood goal was to be a talk-show host. In 1967, he began as the sidekick on *The Joey Bishop Show*, but lost his job when *The Tonight Show* trounced Bishop in the ratings. In 1975, Philbin hosted his first game show, *The Neighbors*.
> Comedian Groucho Marx took a turn as a game-show host in 1947. With his film career stalling, he was hired to host a radio show called *You Bet Your Life*. The show was designed to highlight Marx's witty humor, but most of his ad-libs were actually scripted. It eventually became one of early TV's biggest hits.
> Joe Trela, age 25, became the youngest winner to date on American TV's *Who Wants to Be a Millionaire?* in March 2000. One question about baseball took Trela 15 minutes to correctly answer—shy of the then-record of 17 minutes; the aired sequence was edited to under five minutes.

Who Knew?

> Rod Serling wrote the script for *Planet of the Apes*.
> Dennis Franz *(NYPD Blue)* was the manager of the Bates Motel in *Psycho 2*.
> TV news personality Jane Pauley is married to *Doonesbury* cartoonist Garry Trudeau.
> The television spy series *Get Smart* released a movie sequel called *The Nude Bomb*.
> *All in the Family* cast member Sally Struthers appeared in the film *Five Easy Pieces* with Jack Nicholson.

Course 1096: **You're an Animal?**

> Lassie was played by several male dogs, despite the female name, because male collies were thought to look better on camera. The main "actor" was named Pal.
> In the 1950s, TV and film star collie Lassie's salary was $5,000 per week.
> On *Sesame Street*, one man—Carroll Spinney—plays Big Bird *and* Oscar the Grouch. From within the 8' 2" yellow feathered suit, Spinney watches a small monitor with the same view as the audience. He operates Big Bird's head with one hand while working the bird's hand with the other. When Oscar and Big Bird are in the same scene, Spinney speaks for both Muppets, while another puppeteer operates Oscar.
> When *Sesame Street*'s Big Bird visited the Nixon White House as a guest of First Lady Patricia Nixon, the Secret Service's radio frequency got mixed up with Big Bird's microphone frequency—so the Secret Service was picking up Big Bird's lines in their earpieces.

Jay Silverheels was Tonto on TV's *The Lone Ranger*. After the series concluded, he became a successful horse breeder and racer. When asked if he would ever consider racing Scout, Tonto's famous horse, Silverheels replied, "Heck, even I can beat Scout!"

> Television horse Mr. Ed was foaled in 1949 in El Monte, California. Mr. Ed's original name was Bamboo Harvester. Raised as a parade and show horse, he was once owned by the president of the California Palomino Society. He died in Tahlequah, Oklahoma, on February 28, 1979, at age 30.

Course 1099: On TV and Off

> "If it weren't for Philo T. Farnsworth, inventor of the television, we'd still be eating frozen radio dinners."—Johnny Carson

> "This is by far the largest group of radio and television correspondents ever assembled this far from a Los Angeles courtroom."—Bill Clinton

> "Television is the first truly democratic culture—the first culture available to everyone and entirely governed by what the people want. The most terrifying thing is what people do want."—Clive Barnes

"Television is an invention that permits you to be entertained in your living room by people you would not have in your home."—David Frost

> "If it weren't for electricity, we'd all be watching television by candlelight."—George Gobel

> "Television brought the brutality of war into the comfort of the living room. Vietnam was lost in the living rooms of America—not on the battlefields of Vietnam."—Marshall Herbert McLuhan

> "Good heavens, television is something you appear on; you don't watch."—Noel Coward

> "I hate television. I hate it as much as peanuts. But I can't stop eating peanuts."—Orson Welles

"It is difficult to produce a television documentary that is both incisive and probing when every twelve minutes one is interrupted by twelve dancing rabbits singing about toilet paper."—Rod Serling

Yo-ho-ho and a Bottle of—

During its debut 2000 season, the island location used for TV's *Survivor* was a staging post for modern-day pirates. These pirates, with high-tech speedboats, used the remote island for international black marketeering. In retaliation for the invasion of their privacy by the Hollywood crew, several bad guys one day chased the show's creator, Mark Burnett, in their speedboat. Burnett later said he feared he would be killed. No such luck.

Final Exam

1. Before they ever became president, Harry Truman, John F. Kennedy, Richard Nixon, and Herbert Hoover were all seen on live TV.

True or False?

2. Actor Alan Alda, who played the sardonic Hawkeye Pierce on *M*A*S*H,* was the only member of the television show cast who actually served as a soldier in the Korean War.

True or False?

3. The name of a master of ceremonies on a TV awards show is technically a *symposiarch.*

True or False?

4. Talk-show host Conan O'Brien's stepfather was once the lieutenant governor of the state of Delaware.

True or False?

5. A *claque* is a group of people hired to applaud an act or performer.

True or False?

6. The late hippie-crooner Tiny Tim (whose marriage ceremony on *The Tonight Show* to Miss Vicki was one of the highest-rated programs in TV history) had body odor so vile that Carson got nauseous several times.

True or False?

7. Comedian George Carlin was thrown off *The Ed Sullivan Show* for making an obscene gesture to Ed.

True or False?

8. Six years before starring in *Xena: Warrior Princess,* Lucy Lawless was disqualified from a beauty contest for using obscenities, which were picked up by a mike that she was still wearing and broadcast to millions.

True or False?

9. "Kemo Sabe," the words used by Tonto to address the Lone Ranger, means "White Brother."

True or False?

10. Lou Grant was the only character *not* fired in the final episode of *The Mary Tyler Moore Show.*

True or False?

ANSWERS

1. TRUE. Did you think we were trying to trick you with Herbert Hoover? You are so wrong! The first successful long-distance demonstration of TV took place in the United States way back in the year 1927. Then-secretary of commerce Herbert Hoover (who would become President Hoover in 1929) made a speech in Washington, which was seen and heard on a television in New York City.

2. FALSE. The Korean War veteran was Jamie Farr, who played the outrageous cross-dressing Corporal Max Klinger on the TV sitcom. He wore size-10 pumps.

3. TRUE.

4. FALSE. His *real* father is Dr. Thomas O'Brien, a noted epidemiologist, the head of microbiology at Peter Brigham Hospital, and a professor at Harvard Medical School. His mother, Ruth Reardon O'Brien, was a partner at Ropes and Gray law firm outside Boston until her 1997 retirement.

5. TRUE.

6. FALSE. According to sources, Tiny Tim took at least eight baths a day. He was obsessed with germs and cleanliness, and went so far as to avoid eating off china plates and using standard utensils. He didn't believe that germs could be completely washed away, and so always requested paper plates and plastic forks, spoons, and knives when eating—even when in public.

7. FALSE. Carlin actually appeared on the show eleven times. It was comedian Jackie Mason who gave Ed the finger!

8. FALSE. Lucy Lawless was crowned Mrs. New Zealand in 1989, without incident.

9. FALSE. They mean "Trusty Scout."

10. FALSE. It was Ted Baxter.

4

The USELESS
School of
Biology

Featuring the Psychology Institute

Wasn't biology class a total waste? Didn't you get the feeling that your teachers left all the really good stuff out? Well trust us, they did! They were too busy teaching you all that Useful Knowledge (i.e. normal body temperature is 98.6 degrees, red blood cells carry oxygen, your brain is where all memories are stored, etc.) But they never mentioned that a man's brain is only 2 percent of his body weight, while a woman's brain makes up 2.5 percent of her body weight—a full 25 percent more. Hence, women are heavier thinkers.

They may have taught you that a normal person has two vocal cords. But they probably skipped over the fact that people also have two false vocal cords, which have no direct role in producing sound. Your biology teacher may have discussed the harmful effects of staying out in the sun, yet failed to mention that the skin that peels off after a bad sunburn is called *blype*.

What's worse, when it finally came to human reproduction, all you ever got was the standard lecture about the sperm and the egg. Never once did your teachers discuss the psychological research showing that Protestants and Jews married to Catholics have sex far more frequently than those wed to members of their own faith. Indeed, while your instructors may have touched upon all the muscles involved in kissing, we bet they never informed you that what is called a French kiss in England and America is known as an English kiss in France.

Alright, there's literally a body of Useless Knowledge here. Let's see how fast your brain can ingest it!

Course 809: **Gray Matters**

> A bowl of lime Jell-O, when hooked up to an EKG machine, exhibited movements virtually identical to the brain waves of a healthy adult man or woman.
> What you think is so superficial. The brain gets its intelligence from a surface layer of tissue no more than a quarter of an inch thick. Called gray matter, it contains about 8 billion nerve cells interlinked by some 10,000 miles of nerve fibers for each cubic inch.

Think that being called a Neanderthal is an insult? Neanderthal man, the first human being in the true sense, had a brain capacity 100 cubic centimeters larger than modern man's (or woman's).

> The brain comprises about 2 percent of a person's total body weight. Yet it requires 25 percent of all oxygen used by the body, as opposed to the 12 percent used by the kidneys and the 7 percent used by the heart.

- The brain is surrounded by a membrane containing veins and arteries. This membrane is filled with nerves of feeling. However, the brain itself has no feeling; if it is cut with a scalpel, the person feels no pain.
- Britney Spears take note: it's all downhill after 20, when your brain reaches its maximum weight of about 3 pounds. Over the next 60 years, as billions of nerve cells die within the brain, it loses about 3 ounces. The brain begins to lose cells at a rate of 50,000 per day by the age of 30.
- You definitely have water on the brain. The human brain is 74 percent water.

Enjoy those reruns of *Gilligan's Island*? Your brain is actually more active while you are sleeping than it is while you are watching TV.

- AT&T, eat your heart out. In one day, the human brain generates more electrical impulses than all the telephones in the world put together. The nerve impulses can travel as fast as 170 mph.
- It may be possible to attend your own funeral. The human brain continues sending out electrical wave signals for up to 37 hours following death.

The fingernails grow faster on the hand you favor. If you are right-handed, your right fingernails will grow faster, and vice versa. The middle fingernail grows faster than any other nail.

Advanced Study: **Anatomy of a Booger**

A booger is made of a piece of dried nasal mucus or snot. Mucus is the thin, slippery material that is found inside your nose.

Your nose makes nearly a cupful of snot every day through the mucous membranes in the nose. When you inhale air, it contains lots of tiny particles like dust, dirt, germs, and pollen. If these particles made it to the lungs, the lungs could get damaged, and it would be difficult to breathe. Snot works by trapping these particles.

After these particles get stuck inside the nose, the mucus surrounds them along with some of the tiny hairs inside the nose called *cilia*. The mucus dries around the particles. When these clump together, you're left with a booger! Boogers can be squishy and slimy or tough and crumbly.

Course 869: **Introduction to Sex**

- Our advice is to take a cold shower *before* sex. Cold showers actually increase sexual arousal.

Do you love New York? Following a 20-year study, a fertility specialist, Dr. Harry Fisch, reported in 1996 that Big Apple men have higher sperm counts and better semen quality than men of Los Angeles. Experts believe the warm weather and higher pollution in Los Angeles might be the culprit behind the lower quality.

> So much for hot sex. A recent study purports there are fewer births nine months after a heat wave. It found that an increase of about 21.60° Fahrenheit in summer temperatures reduces births the following spring by up to 6 percent. Researchers at the Kinsey Institute for Sex Research concluded that high temperatures could reduce people's sense of well-being, which could result in a reduction in sexual interest. Another study found lower sperm counts and higher rates of miscarriage during hot weather.

> Quaaludes, the sex drug of choice during the disco era, were first developed to fight malaria.

> A person who has an irrational fear of childbirth can be said to be either *maieusiophobic* or *tocophobic*.

Is the thought of having kids stressful? A survey conducted at Iowa State College in 1969 suggested that a parent's stress at the time of a baby's conception plays a major role in determining that baby's sex. The child tended to be of the same sex as the parent who was under less stress.

> Does marriage stink? A Swiss study found that a majority of women unconsciously choose mates with a body odor that differs from their own natural scents, which, as a result, ensures better immune protection for their children. *Longevity* magazine reported that the genes that battle disease-provoking substances also influence body odor.

> One-fourth of the people who lose their sense of smell also lose their desire for sexual relations.

> Men can have 8 million genetically different sperm, and women a like number of egg types. Together they can produce 64 billion children with no genetic duplicates.

Is he a strong lover? Men who take steroids to build muscles are believed to have extremely low sperm counts. So reported a British Center of Reproductive Medicine study, which revealed that, after giving up steroids, it takes 1–3 years for a man to recover enough to father a child.

> All the genetic material in the sperm and egg cells that produced the Earth's present population could fit into a space the size of an aspirin.

> Relative to its tiny size, the human sperm cell can swim 50 percent faster than an adult male can.
> The largest cell in the human body is the female ovum, or egg cell. It is about 1/180 inch in diameter. The smallest cell in the human body is the male sperm. It takes about 175,000 sperm cells to weigh as much as a single egg cell. Hence, even in the beginning, women have more substance than men.

THE DUALITY OF THE PENIS

Is it possible to double your pleasure? In 1609, a doctor by the name of Wecker discovered a corpse in Bologna that had two penises. Since his findings, researchers have recorded eighty other official cases of men who were so endowed. Maybe the doctor should have changed his name to Pecker.

Course 861: Oh, Baby!

(Prerequisite: Course 969: Introduction to Sex)

> A 3-week-old embryo is no larger than a sesame seed. The body of a 1-month-old fetus is no heavier than an envelope and a sheet of paper. Its hand is no larger than a teardrop.
> A human fetus acquires fingerprints only after three months in the womb.

Babies are born with 300 bones, but by adulthood, we have only 206 in our bodies.

> Babies are born without kneecaps; they don't appear until the ages of 2–6 months old.
> Babies have taste buds all over the insides of their mouths, not just on their tongues. Adults and children have no taste buds on the center of their tongues.
> Most newborns cry without tears until they are 3–6 weeks old.

When the female embryo is only 6 weeks old, it makes preparations for motherhood by developing egg cells. When the baby girl is born, each of her ovaries carries about 1 million egg cells—all that she will ever have.

> A 4-month-old fetus will startle and turn away if a bright light is flashed on its mother's belly. Babies in the womb will also react to sudden loud noises, even if their mother's ears are muffled.

> Of all the senses, babies' sense of smell is the strongest, enabling them to recognize their mothers by scent.

For Women Only

A woman's arthritic pains will almost always disappear as soon as she becomes pregnant.

During menstruation, the sensitivity of a woman's middle finger is reduced. Medical science has yet to explain why.

Course 823: **How Long Is It?**

> Each cell in the human body has an estimated 8 feet of DNA.
> If laid out in a straight line, the average adult's blood vessels would be nearly 60,000 miles long—enough to circle Earth 2½ times. The heart pumps blood through this labyrinth and back again once every minute.

If one were to unravel the entire human alimentary canal (esophagus, stomach, large and small intestines), it would reach the height of a 3-story building.

> One square inch of skin on the human hand contains some 72 feet of nerve fiber. In the adult human body, there are 46 miles of nerves.
> The kidney consists of over 1 million little tubes, and the total length of the tubes in both kidneys runs to about 40 miles.
> The *epididymis*, the tube that carries spermatozoa, is 15 to 20 feet long in an adult male. Luckily, this rarely affects the length of the penis.

Do You Have a Radiant Smile?

False teeth are often radioactive. Approximately 1 million Americans wear some form of denture; half of these dentures are made of a porcelain compound laced with minute amounts of uranium to stimulate fluorescence. Without the uranium additive, the dentures would be a dull green color when seen under artificial light.

Course 807: **The Average Human**

> The average adult eyeball weighs about one ounce.
> The lungs of an average adult, unfolded and flattened out, would cover an area the size of a tennis court.

THE AVERAGE HUMAN BODY HOLDS ENOUGH...

sulfur to kill all the fleas on an average dog.

potassium to fire a toy cannon.

carbon to make 900 pencils.

fat to make 7 bars of soap.

water to distill 10 gallons.

phosphorous to make 2,200 match heads.

> The average person's total skin covering would weigh about 6 pounds if collected in one mass.
> By the age of 20, the average man or woman has lost up to 20 percent of his or her sense of smell. By the age 60, 60 percent is gone.
> The average person who stops smoking requires 1 hour less sleep a night.
> There are about 2 million sweat glands in the average human body. The average adult loses 540 calories with every liter of sweat. An average man on an average day excretes 2½ quarts of sweat.

The average lifespan of our taste buds is 7 to 10 days. The average human eyelash lives about 150 days.

HOW HOT ARE YOU?

Pound for pound, the human body produces 5 times more heat than the sun. The production of heat from the sun averages only 2 calories per pound of its mass daily, while the typical human body generates 10 calories per pound of mass each day.

COURSE 878: **Matters of the Heart**

> The human heart creates enough pressure when it pumps out to the body to squirt blood 30 feet.

> The human heart grows by enlargement of cells, not by cell multiplication. A baby's heart is $1/16$ the size of an adult's, but contains the same number of cells.
> The human heart is no bigger than a fist and yet is wrapped in so much muscle that it can continue pumping even if a third of its muscle mass is destroyed.

The human heart rests between beats. In the average lifetime of 70 years, the total resting time is estimated to be about 40 years.

> The valves of the human heart are as thick as a single piece of tissue paper.
> Women reject heart transplants more often than men.
> In 1 hour, your heart produces enough energy to raise almost 1 ton of weight a yard off the ground, and it beats 40 million times in a year.
> In 1 year, the average human heart circulates from 770,000 to 1.6 million gallons of blood through the body. This is enough fluid to fill 200 tank cars, each with a capacity of 8,000 gallons.

Using the electric chair could be overkill, since it only takes 15 watts of electricity going through a human body to stop the heart. Common lightbulbs run on about 25 to 75 watts of electricity. So come on, let's try to conserve energy!

Can You Stomach This?

Every 3 days, your body makes a new protective lining for your stomach. Without it, the stomach would literally eat itself alive in about 2 weeks. The hydrochloric acid of the human digestive process is so powerful a corrosive that it easily can burn its way through a cotton handkerchief, and even penetrate the iron of an automobile body. Yet, it doesn't endanger the stomach's sticky mucous walls.

Course 892: The Fart on a Molecular Level

> The scientific name for a fart is *flatus* or *flatulence*.
> A fart is a combination of gases (nitrogen, carbon dioxide, oxygen, methane, and hydrogen sulfide) that travels from a person's stomach to their anus.
> The gas that makes farts stink is hydrogen sulfide. This gas contains sulfur, which causes farts to have a smelly odor. The more sulfur-rich your diet, the more your farts will stink. Some of the foods that cause really smelly farts are beans, cabbage, cheese, soda, and eggs.

On the average, a healthy person farts 16 times a day. As a matter of fact, females fart just as much as males.

> It is estimated that a healthy individual release 3.5 oz. of gas in a single flatulent emission—or about 17 oz. in a day.
> Farts that contain a large amount of methane and hydrogen can be very flammable.
> People fart the most in their sleep, particularly if they went to Taco Bell.

In the animal kingdom, the animals that fart the most are the elephants.

Goose Bumps: **A Historical Perspective**

The gooseflesh you get when you're cold is the body's attempt to erect the coat of hair our ancestors lost 100,000 years ago. When an animal's fur stands on end, the expanded air layer between the skin and the fur surface insulates the body.

When it's hot and you need to cool down, little muscles at the base of each hair relax. Your hair becomes relaxed. Your sweat glands pump out body heat in sweat. Your blood vessels get big to take more heat to the skin in order to get rid of it. But when it's cold, the arrector muscle pulls the hair up. The duct to the sweat glands gets small to conserve heat. Our blood vessels also get small to save heat.

Humans don't have very much hair on their bodies anymore (except maybe for guys who get their backs waxed). So, hair standing up doesn't make very good insulation—we don't have enough fur for that. However, those little muscles we have on the end of each hair still work. They still make goose bumps.

The USELESS Psychology Institute

On the psychology front, while you may know that *agoraphobia* is the fear of leaving home, so does everyone else. Replace that Useful Knowledge with a phobia that's far more common—the fear of returning home, No, it's not called homophobia; it's called *nostophobia*. Lots of authors suffer from nostophobia, especially the fear of returning home and having to write a book chapter before their publisher asks for the advance back.

To be ultra politically correct, say that, following the impeachment and the Florida election fiasco, you are now suffering from *politicophobia*, a terror experienced when exposed to politicians. By the way, hopefully you are able to share this book's insights with someone you truly love, and don't suffer from *anuptaphobia*—the horrible fear of staying single.

And should you find this all very amusing, be thankful that you don't have *cherophobia*, which is the obsessive dread of laughing to death. Isn't it obvious by now? Your study of human psychology has been woefully lacking—a serious condition that we intend to remedy with the following useless course study.

Course 854: **Hyper Hypochondria**

> **Severe Blinking:** Extreme winking of the eyes might be early evidence of *blepharospasm*, a muscle dysfunction that forces the eyelids to stay locked shut for the rest of your life.
> **Hairs in the Brush:** A symptom that could indicate *alopecia universalis*, a stress-induced malady. This disorder not only causes all the hair on your head to fall out, but chest hair, leg hair, pubic hair and hair anywhere else on your body to fall out—underarms too!
> **Smelly Body:** The medical diagnosis could read *trimethylaminuria* (the fish-odor syndrome). Most characteristic of this condition is a noxious and stubborn body odor reminiscent of rotten flounder.

Excessive Diarrhea: It may be the first sign of *Ebola* virus infection. If so, the severity of this condition will quickly escalate, and within a few days every orifice on your body will be gushing blood profusely.

> **Deep Hunger:** It might point to an unusual eating disorder called *tomatophagia*. People with tomatophagia develop unusual cravings for such things as tomatoes, ice, detergent, starch, clay, and even dirt.
> **Little Wrinkles:** Those crinkles could signal the early onset of *progeria*, a disorder that produces dramatic signs of premature aging. Cells literally stop replacing themselves; total baldness can result in just a few months, as well as gray hair, yellowish nails, and drooping, deeply creased skin.
> **Unusual Itchiness:** Perhaps its a sign of *Streptococcus-A*, better known as flesh-eating bacteria. Should this be the case, then death will follow in just a few more days, as the disease consumes every shred of skin on your body, exposing your internal organs.

Intense Headache: If it's *mad cow disease* then, as you're reading this page, highly virulent bacteria are demolishing your central nervous system while converting your brain tissue to porous jelly.

Phobia	Fear of...
alektorophobia	chickens
allodoxaphobia	opinions
athazagoraphobia	being forgotten or ignored
coprastasophobia	constipation
coulrophobia	clowns
dentophobia:	dentists
dishabiliophobia	undressing in front of someone
Francophobia	France, french culture
hadephobia	hell
hippopotomonstroses and quippedaliophobia	long words
homilophobia	sermons
liticaphobia	lawsuits
meteorophobia	meteors
metrophobia	poetry
novercaphobia	step-mothers
obesophobia	gaining weight
ouranophobia	heaven
paraskavedekatriaphobia	Friday the 13th
peladophobia	bald people
pteronophobia	being tickled by feathers
sinistrophobia	people who are left-handed
syngenesophobia	relatives
triskaidekaphobia	the number thirteen
venustraphobia	beautiful women

The psychology department of Dayton University reports that loud talk can be ten times more distracting than the sound of a jackhammer. Loud, incessant chatter can make a listener nervous and irritable, and even start him on the road to insanity.

Course 855: **Exotic or Neurotic?**

> Poet and story writer Edgar Allan Poe was expelled from West Point, the U.S. military academy, because he showed up for a parade in his birthday suit.
> Hans Christian Andersen, immortalized for his famous fairy tales, was considered an ugly child and had no friends, so he lived in a dream world as a boy. (Not helping Hans's mental state in later life was the fact that his fairy tales were greeted by scathing reviews: "...quite unsuitable for children...positively harmful for the mind..." etc.)

Beethoven poured cold water over his head when he sat down to compose music, believing that it stimulated his brain's creative process.

> A tenth-century grand vizier of Persia took his entire library with him wherever he went. The 117,000-volume library was carried by camels trained to walk in alphabetical order.
> As valedictorian for her high school, actress Jodie Foster delivered her graduation speech in French.

Should members of these actual clubs be considered slightly deranged: Committee for Immediate Nuclear War, the National Society for Prevention of Cruelty to Mushrooms, the Order of Manly Men, and our favorite, the Institute of Totally Useless Skills?

> Country star Lyle Lovett reportedly is afraid of cows.

Henry Ford was obsessed with soybeans. He once wore a suit and tie made from soy-based material, served a 16-course meal made entirely from soybeans, and ordered many Ford auto parts to be made from soy-derived plastic.

> Floor-cleaning products in Venezuela have ten times the pine fragrance of U.S. floor cleaners. Venezuelan women won't buy a weaker fragrance. These obsessive homemakers may wet-mop their tile floors twice a day, leaving windows and doors open so the scent can waft out to the street to send the message that their houses are clean.

> In 1939, Ernest Vincent Wright wrote a novel titled *Gadsby*. Its 267 pages and 50,000 words do not contain a single letter "e."

Singer Aretha Franklin has an extreme fear of flying. She won't travel on airplanes, even for concerts clear across the country.

> Tennis champ André Agassi has a spider phobia, according to Brooke Shields in a statement she made to the press in October 1996.
> Nearly a quarter of all U.S. pet owners bring their pet to their jobs. Last June, 200 American companies participated in the first-ever Take Your Dog to Work Day.

Goodfellows Insurance outfit in London capitalizes on many people's weird mental states. Among the most requested policies are the "Alien All Risks" package, which offers $1.7 million coverage for just $400 dollar a year, should someone be abducted or impregnated by something not of this Earth.

To date, 40,000 people have paid for this sense of security. Back in 1999, the ingenious company sold 15,000 women— terrified that they might unwillingly be forced to give birth to the messiah—immaculate contraception protection.

Napoleonic Complexes?

Celebrities who measure 5' 3" or less include...

Linda Hunt: 4' 9"	Joan Rivers: 5' 2"
Janis Ian: 4' 10"	Linda Ronstadt: 5' 2"
Dolly Parton: 4' 11"	Paul Simon: 5' 2"
Petula Clark: 5' 0"	Loretta Lynn: 5' 2"
Shari Lewis: 5' 0"	Sissy Spacek: 5' 2"
Danny DeVito: 5' 0"	Shirley Temple Black: 5' 3"
Paul Williams: 5' 0"	Truman Capote: 5' 3"
Paul Anka: 5' 0"	Sammy Davis, Jr.: 5' 3"
Carrie Fisher: 5' 1"	Bo Derek: 5' 3"
Janeane Garofalo: 5' 1"	Judy Garland: 5' 3"
Bette Midler: 5' 1"	Sarah Michelle Gellar: 5' 3"
Stevie Nicks: 5' 1"	Dorothy Hamill: 5' 3"

Natalie Wood: 5' 1"

Sally Struthers: 5' 1"

Paula Abdul: 5' 2"

Linda Blair: 5' 2"

Sally Field: 5' 2"

Jennifer Love Hewitt: 5' 2"

Alyssa Milano: 5' 2"

Sarah Jessica Parker: 5' 2"

Deborah Harry: 5' 3"

Davy Jones: 5' 3"

Jennifer Jason Leigh: 5' 3"

Hayley Mills: 5' 3"

Jane Pauley: 5' 3"

Bernadette Peters: 5' 3"

Lisa Marie Presley: 5' 3"

Mickey Rooney: 5' 3"

The science of determining psychological traits by examining a person's shoes is *scarpology*.

Course 856: **Life-and-Death Issues**

> Alexander the Great's remains were preserved in a huge crock of honey. Among the ancient Egyptians, it was common practice to bury the dead in this manner.

> To keep a corpse's lips shut, undertakers pass a suture through the nasal septum and tie it to the lower lip. Sometimes they use an injector needle gun to place wires into the lower and upper jaws; the wires are then twisted together to close the mouth.

> Residents of Hawaii outlive residents of all other states. Louisianans are the most prone in the United States to die an early death.

Undertakers report that human bodies do not deteriorate as quickly as they used to. The reason, they believe, is that the modern diet contains so many preservatives that these chemicals tend to prevent the body from decomposing too rapidly after death.

> Humphrey Bogart's ashes are in an urn that also contains a small gold whistle. Lauren Bacall had the whistle inscribed "If you need anything, just whistle"—the words she spoke to him in their first film together, *To Have and Have Not.*

> Famous American showman P. T. Barnum had his obituary published before his death.

> Pablo Picasso was stillborn. The midwife left him on a table. Picasso's uncle brought him to life with a lung-full of cigar smoke.

> Francis Bacon (1561–1626), the Elizabethan champion of the scientific method, died in pursuit of a better way of preserving food. He caught a severe cold while attempting to preserve a chicken by filling it with snow.
> From the 1850s to the 1880s, the most common cause of death among cowboys in the American West was being dragged by a horse while caught in the stirrups.

John F. Kennedy, Lee Harvey Oswald, and Jack Ruby all have one thing in common: they share the same place of death— Parkland Memorial Hospital in Dallas, Texas. Ruby, convicted murderer of Oswald, died on January 3, 1967, from a blood clot that lodged in his lungs. He was suffering from lung cancer.

> Lee Harvey Oswald's cadaver tag sold at an auction for $6,600 in 1992.
> Robert Capa, legendary photojournalist who captured the most famous photos of D day, was once quoted as saying, "If your pictures aren't good enough, you're not close enough." He walked his talk until his death, when he stepped on a land mine in the French-Indonesian War.
> John "Pop" Reed, a stagehand at Philadelphia's Walnut Street Theater, left instructions that his skull was to be used as Yorick's skull in productions of *Hamlet*. His desire was carried out, and he posthumously played Yorick for years. Today his skull resides at the Van Pelt Library of the University of Pennsylvania.

Since 1978, at least 37 people have died as a result of shaking vending machines in an attempt to get free merchandise. More than 100 have been injured.

> In a recent 5-year period, 24 residents of Tokyo died while bowing to other people.
> Mr. P. J. Tierney, father of the modern diner, died of indigestion in 1917 after eating at a diner.
> Jefferson County, Kentucky, announced in 1996 that it was going to reduce its pauper burial system to restrain the tide of indigents who came to the county just to die. According to officials, the cost per pauper burial was almost $700.

In 1980, the *Yellow Pages* accidentally listed a Texas funeral home under "Frozen Foods."

AFTERLIFE INSURANCE?

Japan's Buddhist establishment has been under attack over the practice of charging bereaved, vulnerable relatives huge fees for afterlife names given to the dead at their funerals. The tradition is centuries-old, and began with names being conferred only on Buddhist priests.

When temples began granting afterlife names to common people, the names became something akin to a ranking system, reflecting the deceased's noble actions during life. The highest rank, called *ingo*, costs more than $8,300. Of the average $5,300 paid to temples for Tokyo funeral fees, about $3,300 goes for the posthumous name. Talk about making a killing!

ORGANIC DATA

Even if the stomach, the spleen, 80 percent of the intestines, one kidney, one lung, and virtually every organ from the pelvic and groin area are removed, the human body can still survive.

And even if 80 percent of your liver were removed, the remaining part would continue to function. Within a few months, the liver would have reconstituted itself to its original size!

Course 865: On the Medical Charts

> Zeppo Marx of Marx Brothers fame owned a patent for a wristwatch with a heart monitor.
> Arthur Conan Doyle, author of the Sherlock Holmes stories, was an ophthalmologist by profession.
> A heart attack most often occurs in the morning, when mental and physical stress are at their peak.

Queen Victoria's physicians prescribed marijuana to relieve her menstrual cramps.

> A study by researcher Frank Hu and the Harvard School of Public Health found that women who snore are at an increased risk of high blood pressure and cardiovascular disease.
> Banging your head against a wall can burn up to 150 calories per hour.
> Aristotle believed the main purpose of the human brain was to cool the blood.

In the spring of 2000, it was reported that a 25-year-old Tehran transsexual, who had just undergone extensive surgery to become a woman, said he wanted to change back to a man after realizing just how poorly women are treated in Iran.

> Girl Scout founder Juliette Gordon Low was nearly deaf. A grain of rice thrown at her 1886 wedding lodged in her ear, and the resulting infection destroyed most of her hearing in that ear. Her other ear also had diminished ability.

> Helen Keller (1880–1968), blind and deaf from an early age, developed her sense of smell so well that she could identify friends by their personal odors.
> According to the founder of Children of Deaf Adults, 90 percent of the children of deaf parents have no hearing loss, and it is not unusual for a hearing child to suspect that his or her deaf parents are faking deafness.

A study of American coins and currency revealed the presence of bacteria, including staphylococcus and *E. coli* on 18 percent of the coins and 7 percent of the bills.

> Huckleberry Finn's remedy for warts was swinging a dead cat in a graveyard at night.
> The first contraceptive diaphragms, used centuries ago, were citrus rinds.

Brain Drains and Gains

More than 100 years ago, the felt hat makers of England used mercury to stabilize wool. Most of them eventually were poisoned by the fumes, as demonstrated by the Mad Hatter in Lewis Carroll's *Alice in Wonderland*. Breathing mercury fumes over time will cause *erethism*, a disorder characterized by nervousness, irritability, and strange personality changes.

According to a British medical report, the fungi that feed on old paper may be mildly hallucinogenic, and the "fungal hallucinogens" may cause an "enhancement of enlightenment" in readers. The source of creative inspiration for many great authors through history may have been a quick sniff of moldy books, causing them to get high.

Course 873: **The Eyes Have It**

> The only part of the human body that has no blood supply is the cornea in the eye. It takes in oxygen directly from the air.
> It takes the human eyes an hour to adapt completely to seeing in the dark. Once adapted, however, the eyes are about 100,000 times more sensitive to light than they are in bright sunlight.
> The average person blinks 25 times per minute, which works out to about 13,140,000 blinks each year.
> The sensitivity of the human eye is so keen that on a clear, moonless night, a person with 20/20 vision standing on a mountain can see a match being struck as far as 50 miles away. Much to their amazement, astronauts in orbit were able to see the wakes of ships.

A bird's eye takes up about 50 percent of its head; our eyes take up about 5 percent of our head. To be comparable to a bird's eyes, the eyes of a human being would have to be the size of baseballs.

> The human eyes can perceive more than 1 million simultaneous visual impressions and are able to discriminate among nearly 8 million gradations of color.
> Poker players take note: the pupil of the eye expands as much as 45 percent when a person looks at something pleasing.
> Visual scientist have estimated that, by the age of 60, our eyes have been exposed to more light energy than would be released by a nuclear blast.
> The rapid, irregular eye movement that occurs when changing focus from one point to another, as while reading or looking out from a moving train, is called *saccade*.

The iris of the human eye provides better personal identification than a fingerprint. A scan of the iris reveals 256 different characteristics. A fingerprint has only 40. So here's looking at you!

No Bones About It

The strongest bone in the body, the thigh bone, is hollow. Ounce for ounce, it has a greater pressure tolerance and bearing strength than a rod of equivalent size in cast steel. When an average adult is walking, his weight puts a downward pressure of 12,000 pounds per square inch on each thighbone. In this case, even the thinnest part of the thighbone, at 1-inch thick, supports the weight of a male African elephant.

Course 882: **What's in a Name?**

> The little lump of flesh just forward of your ear canal, right next to your temple, is called a *tragus*.
> The white part of the top of your fingernail is called the *lunula*.
> The back of the human hand is the *opisthenar*.

Scurf is another word for dandruff.

> The indentation in the middle area between the nose and the upper lip is called the *philtrum*. Ancient Greeks considered this to be one of the body's most erogenous zones.
> *Strabismus* is the condition of a person's eyes going in different directions.

> When you have a black eye, you have a *bilateral periorbital hematoma*.

If you are suffering from *ozostomia*, you are suffering from *halitosis*, or bad breath.

> *Noologists* study the human mind.
> The adjective *metopic* means "of the forehead."
> People who can't see the color red have *protanopia*.
> A *buccula* is a little-used term for a person's double chin.

A *nullipara* is a woman who has never borne a child.

Now Hear This!

Permanent hearing loss can result from prolonged exposure to sounds at 85 decibels (0 decibels is the threshold for hearing). For comparison, a busy street corner is about 80 decibels, a subway train heard from 20 feet is 100 decibels, a jet plane heard from 500 feet is 110 decibels, and loud thunder is 120 decibels.

A rock band amplified at close range is 140 decibels, which is 100 trillion times the hearing threshold and more than 100,000 times as loud as the level necessary to produce permanent hearing loss.

By the way, the African bushman lives in a quiet, remote environment—not unlike Utah—and has no measurable hearing loss even at age 60.

Course 885: **Stick It Out**

> The strongest muscle in the body is not the heart—it's the tongue!

In the latter part of the eighteenth century, Prussian surgeons treated stutterers by snipping off portions of their tongues.

> The human tongue registers bitter tastes 10,000 times more strongly than sweet tastes. And that's the bitter truth!
> Pigs, dogs, and some other animals can taste water, but people cannot. Humans don't actually taste water; they only taste the chemicals and impurities in the water.

Medical experts have observed that people who stutter rarely do so when they are alone or talking to a pet.

ANOTHER WAY TO LICK CRIME?

Tongue prints are as unique as fingerprints. So watch out where you leave them!

Course 890: Things Are Getting Hairy

> The combined strength of all the hairs on one human head (when woven into a rope) can support the weight of about 400 people.
> The hair of an adult man or woman can stretch 25 percent of its length without breaking. If it is less elastic, it is not healthy.

Poliosis (from the Greek word *polios*, meaning "gray" is the graying of the hair. It's caused when pigment cells stop producing melanin.

> Hair grows slowest at night. It's growth speeds up in the morning, slows down in the afternoon, and accelerates again in the evening. Hair grows faster in summer than in winter.
> The dry material left by dead cells is *keratin*, of which hair and nails are composed.

Hair does not continue to grow after death because it requires nourishment from pumping blood. The hair only appears longer because skin pulls away as the body begins to dry out.

BLONDS HAVE MORE...

Natural blonds have more hairs on their heads than redheads or any shade of brunette. A blond has about 120,000 strands of hair, while a redhead has about 30 percent fewer strands—about 80,000. Brunettes are somewhere in between the two.

What's All the Stink About?

The problem begins when bacteria are attracted to the sweat on your feet and start feeding on it. The bacteria's excretion has a strong odor that causes your feet to smell bad. Since each foot has over 250,000 sweat glands in it, and produces over a pint of sweat a day, there's a lot for the bacteria to eat. Shoes and socks even make the situation worse. They trap the sweat, and then the bacteria have their favorite kind of environment: dark and damp, causing them to go into a feeding frenzy.

Bionote: Men's feet smell at least 40 percent worse than women's. So what else is new?

Final Exam

1. It takes more facial muscles to smile than to frown.

True or False?

2. Drinking alcohol raises the body temperature during cold weather.

True or False?

3. Human beings have been proven to fart even more than elephants.

True or False?

4. Ten percent of your body weight would be from microorganisms on your body if you were freeze-dried.

True or False?

5. The substance that human sweat resembles most closely in terms of chemical composition is seawater.

True or False?

6. A person would have to play Ping-Pong for 2 hours to burn enough calories to lose one pound.

True or False?

7. Whispering is less wearing on your voice than a normal speaking tone.

True or False?

8. It has been determined that one brow wrinkle is the result of 200,000 frowns.

True or False?

9. Midgets and dwarfs almost always have normal-sized children, even if both parents are midgets or dwarfs.

True or False?

10. *Salmonella,* referring to the bacteria that enter a person's digestive tract in contaminated food, was first identified and named in 1889 when U.S. Navy sailors got ill after having a salmon dinner together.

True or False?

ANSWERS

1. FALSE. It takes seventeen facial muscles to smile but 42 to frown.

2. FALSE. It lowers body temperature.

3. FALSE. Of all creatures, elephants fart the most.

4. TRUE.

5. FALSE. It's human blood.

6. FALSE. He or she would have to play for 12 hours.

7. FALSE. Both whispering and shouting stretch the vocal cords.

8. TRUE.

9. TRUE.

10. FALSE. The illness has nothing to do with fish. It was named after U.S. pathologist Daniel E. Salmon.

5

The USELESS
School of
Sports

Even if you are a certified jock or jockette, attended college on an athletic scholarship, or spent the last 27 years watching everything from the Superbowl to *Celebrity Bowling*, your knowledge of useless sports facts is still dismal. You probably have some comprehension of what a goalie does in hockey and know that the sport is played with sticks, but did you know that the very first pucks were made from cow dung? Imagine what they shoved in your face back then during a brawl on the ice!

As a golf enthusiast, you know when to use a putter, a driver, even a three iron. That's all very useful—but okay, wise guy, what golf club did Alan Shepard use on the moon? A six iron—so there! Likewise, baseball fans can spend hours talking about Mark McGwire, Mickey Mantle, and Babe Ruth, but how many of them know that our national sport was not seen first on TV sets in the United States, but in Japan. Yes, sports nuts know all about southpaws and left-handed tennis players and boxers, yet you would never guess that there's actually one sport that *bans* left-handed players entirely—polo.

What about the manly art of self-defense? True devotees may have memorized every statistic about Muhammad Ali and the length of every prison stint served by Mike Tyson and bought every grill George Foreman ever sold, but never in a million years would they know Sonny Liston's major claim to fame. Give up? It turns out the former heavyweight champion was seen on the cover of the Beatles legendary *Sgt. Pepper's Lonely Hearts Club Band* album—with a little help from his friends, of course!

Useless Sports Knowledge will definitely turn your brain to mush—just remember the name Anne Bancroft. Not the famous actress married to Mel Brooks, but the first woman ever to reach the North Pole by dogsled. Need we say more?

Course 403: **Base Principles**

> Not everyone believes that baseball originated in the United States. In 1962, the Soviet newspaper *Izvestia* asserted that *beizbol* was an old Russian game.

> At one time, winning was determined in baseball by which team got 21 runs first. Because it took so long, with players usually wandering off to get drunk, the 21-run-win-game system was soon shelved.

> Vaudevillian Jack Norworth wrote "Take Me Out to the Ballgame" in 1908, after seeing a sign on a bus advertising BASEBALL TODAY/POLO GROUNDS. Norworth and his friend Albert von Tilzer (who wrote the music) had never been to a baseball game before their song became a hit sing-along.

A baseball is the only logo that is not allowed on a major league baseball uniform.

> In 1972, Bernice Gera became baseball's first female professional umpire. Unfortunately, after battling for 5 exhausting years against discriminatory league hotshots and hostile, threatening baseball players, Gera quit, having umped only one game.

> According to the official rules of baseball, no umpire may be replaced during a game unless he is injured or becomes ill. He may also be replaced if he drops dead.

> Chicago's National League baseball franchise has been known by 18 different names establishing a record. They have been the White Stockings, the Colts, the Black Stockings, the Ex-Colts, the Rainmakers, the Orphans, the Cowboys, the Rough Riders, the Desert Rangers, the Pennants, the Recruits, the Zephyrs, the Nationals, the Fourth Nationals, the Third Nationals, the Spuds, and the Trojans. The club owners finally settled on Cubs in 1908, although this hasn't helped them get into a World Series.

Before 1859, baseball umpires were comfortably seated in padded rocking chairs behind home plate.

> Babe Ruth is credited with the invention of the modern baseball bat. He was the first player to order a bat with a knob on the end of the handle, with which he hit 29 home runs in 1919. The company that produced the bat was Louisville Slugger, which has been legendary ever since.

> Baseball Hall of Famers Rogers Hornsby, Gabby Street, and Tris Speaker were members of the Ku Klux Klan. It was also an unconfirmed rumor that Ty Cobb was a member of the KKK.

Eddie Gaedel was the 3'7" midgit who played in only one game for the St. Louis Browns against the Detroit Tigers and who walked on four pitches.

> Baseball legend Ty Cobb amassed a huge fortune from Coca-Cola and General Motors stocks. His net worth at the time of his death was reported to be $11 million. When Cobb entered Emory Hospital in Atlanta near death, he brought with him more than $1 million in negotiable bonds and placed them on the nightstand next to a loaded pistol.

> Baseball's last legal spitball was thrown by Hall of Famer Burleigh Grimes for the New York Yankees in 1934. Although the pitch had been outlawed 14 years earlier, those already throwing it were permitted to continue.

Major league baseball teams buy 182 pounds of special baseball rubbing mud each year from a single farmer in Millsboro, Delaware.

> Five baseball gloves can be made from one cow. The udder isn't used.

> In 1963, baseball pitcher Gaylord Perry said: "They'll put a man on the moon before I hit a home run." Only a few hours after Neil Armstrong set foot on the moon on July 20, 1969, Perry hit the first and only home run of his career.

The National League team in Houston wasn't always called the Astros. They were known originally as the Colt 45s.

> The Brooklyn Dodgers (who later became the Los Angeles Dodgers) did not get their name because of their sporting ability. The term *dodger* was a shortened form of the term *trolley dodgers*, which was first used to describe Brooklynites for their ability to avoid being hit by trolley cars.
> In 1963 Matty, Felipe, and Jesus Alou became the only three brothers in history to start a baseball game in the outfield for the same major league team: the San Francisco Giants.
> In 1965, the minimum annual salary for a baseball player was $6,000, just $1,000 more than it had been in 1947.

Cuban dictator Fidel Castro was once approached by the New York Giants to pitch for them; they had been excited by his pitching prowess during a tour in 1948. His signing bonus would have been $5,000. Had Castro been interested, history may have changed in a major (league) way, with the United States and Cuba playing on the same team!

A PAIGE OF HISTORY

Born Leroy Robert Paige, Satchel Paige was a legend in the Negro Leagues for 29 years. But many of his records were never recorded. On his 42nd birthday, in 1948, he was sold by the Kansas City Monarchs to the Cleveland Indians, and while with that team he became the oldest rookie ever in major league baseball.

Paige also became the first black ever to pitch in the American League, and the fifth to play in the major leagues. As the majors' oldest rookie, Paige had a 6–1 record, mostly in relief, as Cleveland won the 1948 pennant. He also pitched for the St. Louis Browns, and pitched three innings for the Kansas City Athletics in 1965 at the age of 59.

Course 411: **Fouls and Dribbles**

> About 30 percent of NBA players sport tattoos, compared with about 4 percent of the nation's population.
> Basketball got its name from the half-bushel peach baskets used as targets by the originator, James A. Naismith, in 1891.

> A basketball ring's inner diameter is 18 inches.

RARE AIR was the immodest two-word statement on basketball great Michael Jordan's Illinois vanity license plate in the 1990s.

> William Morgan, a student of basketball inventor James Naismith, invented a sport of his own: volleyball.
> Earl Lloyd was the first black ever to play in an NBA game when he took the floor for the Washington Capitols on October 31, 1950, in Rochester, New York. Lloyd was one of three blacks to become NBA players in the 1950 season. The other two were Nat "Sweetwater" Clifton, who was signed by the New York Knicks, and Chuck Cooper, who was drafted by the Boston Celtics. Cooper debuted the night after Lloyd.

In 1966, Wilt Chamberlain become the NBA's all-time leading scorer—on Valentine's Day. Off the court, he probably holds the title of leading scorer as well!

> The Harlem Globetrotters played their unprecedented 20,000th career basketball game on January 12, 1998. No other professional sports team, including the NBA, MLB, NHL, and NFL, has ever reached this historical milestone. The Globetrotters got their start in 1926 as the Savoy Big Five.
> The only NBA team never to earn a pick in the NBA draft lottery is the Utah Jazz.
> Miami Arena Palace of Auburn Hills is the smallest NBA arena.

According to manufacturer Spalding, the average life span of an NBA basketball is 10,000 bounces.

> Until 1937, the referee had to throw a jump ball after every basket.
> In 1974, Moses Malone became the first player to go from high school straight into pro basketball. The move made him the highest-salaried teenage athlete in the United States at that time. Malone was signed by the Utah Stars of the American Basketball Association.
> The NBA's first 7-foot-tall player was Elmore Morgenthaler, who played for Providence in 1946.

A $10,000 fine was promptly issued to Charles Barkley by the NBA for accidentally spitting on an 8-year-old girl.

Course 438: **Lords of the Ring**

> In ancient Greece, a boxing match began with two boxers standing face-to-face, their noses touching. They wore leather thongs embedded with metal studs strapped on their wrists. At one time, metal spikes were added, too. Of course, the sport was still pretty tame compared to Extreme Wrestling.

> Prizefights prior to the turn of the century lasted up to more than a 100 rounds (rounds were often determined by knockdowns). The fighters used bare knuckles (no gloves.) But there were no commercials, so the fights seemed shorter.

> The boxing ring is obviously square—but it used to be a rounded-off area, and the name stuck.

Boxing was the first sport to be filmed. Thomas A. Edison filmed a boxing match between Jack Cushing and Mike Leonard in 1894.

> Former boxing champion Muhammad Ali was the composer of numerous self-admiring verses ("Float like a butterfly, sting like a bee"). He was once invited to lecture on poetry at Oxford University.

> Entertainers who were boxers in the early days of their careers include Roy Clark, Bo Diddley, Bob Hope, John Huston, Martin Lawrence, Ryan O'Neal, and Rod Serling.

Former heavyweight champion George Foreman named all of his 5 sons George.

> Jack Broughton was one of the most revered boxing figures in England. He was entombed at Westminster Abbey, the burial place of British nobility, although he was a commoner.

> In 1876, Nell Saunders defeated Rose Harland in the first U.S. women's boxing match. Saunders received a silver butter dish as a prize.

> Sugar Ray Robinson was the first ex–boxing champion to return from retirement and win back his title. He also became the first boxer to win the middleweight title three times when he knocked out Carl "Bobo" Olson in the second round of their Chicago bout on December 9, 1955.

After his infamous 1997 ear-biting attack on Evander Holyfield, the Hollywood Wax Museum moved boxer Mike Tyson's figure to the Chamber of Horrors right next to the figure of Dr. Hannibal Lecter (from *The Silence of the Lambs*).

BOXING IN BLACK AND WHITE

In June 1946, NBC-TV and Gillette staged what they billed as the first "television sports extravaganza": the Joe Louis–Billy Conn heavyweight fight at Yankee Stadium. The fight was a huge viewing success, with an estimated audience of 150,000 watching on just 5,000 sets. For every TV set tuned in to the fight, there was an average of 30 people watching. Many were seeing a sporting event on television for the first time.

Course 449: Reaching Your Goals

> Until recently, a hockey goaltender never wore a mask. By 1959, Jacques Plante, an NHL All-Star goalie, had accumulated a hairline fracture and 200 stitches. Flying pucks had broken his jaw, both his cheekbones, and his nose. Fibreglass Canada worked with Plante to develop the first-ever hockey goalie mask. While he was wearing the mask, his team, the Montreal Canadiens, won the Stanley Cup for the third time.

> According to the *Detroit Free Press*, 68 percent of professional hockey players have lost at least one tooth.

> According to the National Hockey League, an official hockey puck must be made of vulcanized rubber or another approved material, measure 1 inch thick and 3 inches in diameter, and weigh between 5 and 6 ounces.

The machine that resurfaces the ice on an NHL rink is called a *Zamboni*.

> According to NHL rules, the home team is responsible for providing an adequate supply of official pucks which must be kept in a frozen condition. This supply of pucks must be kept at the penalty bench under the control of one of the regular off-ice officials.

> In hockey, a *butterfly* is a goaltending style in which the goalie keeps his knees together and his feet slightly apart.

> In hockey, a *deke* is a quick fake by a puck carrier, intended to trick an opponent out of position.

In hockey, the penalty box is often referred to as the "sin bin."

> In the 1979–80 season, at age 19, Wayne Gretzky became the youngest hockey player ever to score 50 or more goals and 100 or more points in a season, and the youngest player to be voted Most Valuable Player.

> A 15-foot tall bronze statue stands prominently in front of Edmonton's Northlands Coliseum. It's Wayne Gretzky, of course!

> The prestigious NHL Stanley Cup weighs a whopping 32 pounds.

Course 455: **All You *Don't* Need *Is* Love**

> Using a graphite tennis racket reportedly helps prevent the onset of tennis elbow.

> According to the U.S. Lawn Tennis Association, a tennis ball is supposed to bounce between 53 and 58 inches when it is dropped on concrete from a height of 100 inches. The concrete surface should be 4 inches thick.

In June 1963, the British tennis player Michael Sangster served a ball that was clocked at 154 miles per hour. This is the fastest serve ever documented.

> At age 16, Tracey Austin became the youngest tennis player to win the U.S. Open.

> Martina Hingis of Switzerland won the women's competition in the Australian Open in 1997. At 16, she was the youngest woman to win a Grand-Slam tennis tournament in 110 years.

> Billie Jean King holds the distinction of being the oldest woman to receive a singles seed at Wimbledon. She was 39 years, 209 days old when she got the No. 10 seed in 1983.

> Helen Wills Moody was the first female African-American tennis player to achieve international fame. She had more Wimbledon titles than any woman in history until Martina Navratilova broke the record in 1990.

In 1931, Lili de Alvarez was the first woman to wear shorts at Wimbledon.

> In 1990, John McEnroe, often called "the Brat" because of his infantile on-court behavior, became the first player in 27 years to be disqualified from a Grand Slam tournament for misconduct. His repeated bad manners led to his being booted from the Australian Open.

> To date, the oldest men's singles champion at Wimbledon is Arthur Gore, who won the title in 1909 at age 41 years, 182 days.

This Sport Is Bad!

Badminton is the world's fastest racket sport: a shuttle, commonly known as a *birdie*, can leave the racket at a speed of almost 200 mph. Badminton was first recognized as an official Olympic sport during the 1992 Summer Games. More than 1.1 billion people watched badminton's Olympic debut on TV.

The game as we know it took its name from Badminton House in Gloucestershire, England—home of the duke of Beaufort—and was once known as battledore and also as shuttlecock. Although the sport is not popular in America, crowds of up to 15,000 are common for major badminton tournaments in Malaysia.

The biggest badminton shuttle in the world can be found on the lawns of the Nelson-Atkins Art Museum, in Kansas City—it is 48 times larger than the real thing. This shuttle is 18 feet high and weighing 5,000 pounds.

Famous personalities who play badminton include Paul Newman, when he's not auto racing.

Course 463: **Pedal Pushers**

> The sport with the largest expenses (medical, legal, and others) due to injuries treated in U.S. emergency rooms in 1995 was bicycling, with costs exceeding $4 billion. More than half a million bicycling injuries were documented. A huge percentage of them were head injuries, which could have been prevented had riders worn protective helmets.
> In mountain-biking slang a "snakebite" is a flat tire caused by hitting a hard object. As a result of the impact, the wheel rim pierces the inner tube and creates a two-hole puncture that resembles a snakebite.

American John Howard holds the world record for bicycle speed. In 1985, he reached 245.08 kilometers per hour (about 154 miles per hour) by cycling in the slipstream of a specially designed car.

> Teddy Roosevelt was the police commissioner of New York City in 1895 when he formed the "Bicycle Squad." Members of the squad chased down speeders who exceeded the speed limit of 8 miles per hour.
> Tied at 5 wins each, the top Tour de France winners since the event began in 1903 are Jacques Anquetil (France), Eddy Merckx (Belgium), Bernard Hinault (France), and Miguel Induráin (Spain).

Course 468: **Touchdown!**

> It takes 3,000 cows to supply a single season's worth of footballs for the National Football League.
> Instant replay added a new dimension to televised sports when it was first featured in a 1963 telecast of an Army-Navy football game. In 1964, it became a standard technique on television.
> The men under contract to an NFL team but who don't suit up for games are called the "taxi squad."

Edward Kennedy, brother of JFK and future U.S. senator, scored the only touchdown for Harvard when they played Yale in 1955.

> Gerald Ford was an assistant football coach at Yale. He played football at the University of Michigan and turned down offers to play for the Chicago Bears and the Green Bay Packers. Eventually he tackled the job of being president, but was carried off the field after only one term.

The huddle formation used by football teams originated at Gallaudet University, a Washington, D.C., liberal arts college for deaf people. The purpose was to prevent other schools from reading their sign language.

> In 1906, President Theodore Roosevelt had to call a special meeting of Yale, Harvard, and Princeton representatives at the White House in order to find a way to stop the growing brutality in football. In the previous year 18 Americans lost their lives while playing football, and 154 more were seriously injured. Too bad we don't have the video!
> Theodore Roosevelt also led the Rough Riders, which was comprised of football players, cowboys, and Eastern polo players.
> Actor Dean Cain, the leading man in TV's *Lois and Clark: The New Adventures of Superman,* was signed to play professional football with the Buffalo Bills after his graduation from Princeton. However, he injured his knee three days before his first preseason NFL game. The unfortunate injury forced Cain to pursue a new career.
> Gatorade got its name from the Gators, the University of Florida football team who were the first to test it.

Joe Namath, onetime New York Jets quarterback, donated pantyhose to Planet Hollywood. He wore the pantyhose on the football playing field on chilly days.

> Because of a football's resemblance to an olive, albeit a very large one, the Chinese often call the American game of football "olive ball."
> In 1943, Percy Clark of UCLA made the mistake during the Rose Bowl game of being tackled behind the goal line while attempting to return a punt against Georgia. UCLA lost the game, 2–0. One newspaper carried the headline "CLARK 2, UCLA 0." Clark was openly shunned by classmates, and, in despair, he quit college a week later. He moved to the woods in Oregon, where he spent many years as a recluse; but on a positive note, he did not wind up becoming another Unibomber.

The person who holds second and third place for most yards gained rushing in a single season in the NFL *and* was the first

2000-yard single-season rusher in NFL history is O. J. Simpson. An athlete who has always been a cut above.

THE ORIGIN OF THE HIGH FIVE

In the 1931 Rose Bowl game, Five-Yard Fogerty carried 25 times and gained exactly 5 yards on each carry. It was in that game that teammates celebrated the oddity of Fogerty's feat by slapping palms—the practice now known as exchanging high fives.

Course 471: *Flog* Spelled Backwards

> Golf was banned in England and Scotland in 1457 by King James II because he claimed it distracted people from the archery practice necessary for national defense.
> Americans spend more than $630 million a year on golf balls.
> Before 1850, golf balls were made of leather and stuffed with feathers.

An extremely rare 3 strokes below par on a hole is called an *albatross* or a *double eagle*. A score of either 8 for a hole or 88 for a round is called a *snowman*.

> On the professional golf tour, players are allotted 45 seconds per shot.
> When playing golf, scraping the golf club along the ground before hitting the ball is called *sclaffing*.
> Maricopa County in Arizona boasts the most golf courses in the country, with a reported 168, followed by Palm Beach County in Florida with 150 and Riverside County in California with 145.

A game of golf can be very electrifying—more people are struck by lightning on golf courses than anyplace else, although there's no research on what club most people were using.

> Golfer Arnold Palmer was the first person to make $1 million playing golf.
> Golfing great Ben Hogan's famous reply when asked how to improve one's game was: "Hit the ball closer to the hole."
> A Dolly Parton is a putt on an especially hilly green. It's also known as a roller coaster.

The name of the game may originate from the days of its origins in Scotland, when it was strictly a "Gentlemen Only, Ladies Forbidden" sport—hence GOLF.

> The first outdoor miniature golf courses in the United States were built on rooftops in New York City in 1926.
> The National Golf Association says that, at golf ranges, an extra-large golf-ball bucket contains about 150 balls—90 large balls, 63 medium, and 35 small.

A golfer who found a 203-gram meteorite on the Doon Valley Golf Course near Kitchener, Ontario, on July 12, 1998, was rewarded with a year's worth of free greens fees. The stone had narrowly missed a golfer who was standing near the sixth tee.

> Myrtle Beach, South Carolina, has the most mini-golf courses per area in the United States. At last count, there were 47 in a 60-mile radius.
> While living in Vermont in the 1890s, Rudyard Kipling invented the game of snow golf. He painted his golf balls red so that they could be located in the snow.

WHY DO GOLF BALLS HAVE DIMPLES?

Dimpled golf balls travel up to four times farther than smooth-surfaced golf balls. In the early days, smooth-surfaced balls were used until golfers discovered that old, bumpy balls traveled longer distances.

The science of aerodynamics explains the phenomenon. The dimples reduce the drag on a golf ball by redirecting air pressure behind the golf ball rather than in front of it, changing the levels of pressure by bringing the main airstream very close to the surface of the golf ball. This high-speed airstream near the ball increases the amount of pressure behind the ball—thereby forcing the ball to travel farther. But don't worry: we don't get it, either!

Course 484: **Stable Relationships**

> Horse racing is one of the most ancient sports, originating in central Asia among prehistoric nomadic tribesmen around 4500 B.C. When humans began keeping written records, horse racing was already an organized sport throughout the world. Bookies came much later.
> Since 1940, at least 40 jockeys have died from accidents while racing horses.
> The Kentucky Derby is held at Churchill Downs and is one mile long. The first race held there was in 1875, and Aristides was the winning horse.
> Eddie Arcaro, one of the greatest jockeys in horse-race history, rode 250 losers before he won his first race. Ultimately, Arcaro won 4,779 races—including 5 Derby winners, 6 in the Preakness, and 6 in the Belmont Stakes—on such famous horses as Whirlaway, Citation, and Kelso.

On February 22, 1989, Barbara Jo Rubin became the first female jockey to win a horse race. She rode Cohesian to victory at Charlestown Racetrack in West Virginia. The first woman to ride in the Kentucky Derby was Diane Crump on May 2, 1970.

> Winning "hands down" in horse racing means never once having to use the whip on the animal.
> Horse racing was the first sport to have strict regulations against drugs.

Fillies are permitted to carry 3 to 5 pounds when racing against their male counterparts.

> The standard pitching distance in the game of horseshoes is 40 feet for men and 30 feet for women and juniors.
> In horse racing parlance, a *maiden* is a horse that has yet to run a race; it's not an animal that is still a virgin.

Breakfast of Champions

American consumers were asked to vote for their favorite Wheaties champion of all time. Wheaties celebrated its 75th anniversary in 1999 by rereleasing the original cereal packages featuring the champions selected; the top ten vote recipients were Michael Jordan, Lou Gehrig, Babe Ruth, Mary Lou Retton, Tiger Woods, Cal Ripken, Jr., Walter Payton, John Elway, Jackie Robinson, and the 1980 U.S. Men's Olympic Hockey Team.

Course 490: **Pinned Down**

> Seven thousand years ago, the ancient Egyptians bowled on alleys not unlike our own. They didn't have to rent bowling shoes, however.
> The modern bowling ball was invented in 1862.
> Candlepin bowling uses 10 small pins and 3 balls, and is played primarily in the states of Connecticut and Rhode Island. The ball is only 5 inches in diameter, is made of hard rubber, and has no finger holes.
> Some form of bowling is played in more than 90 countries around the world. Approximately 100 million people participate in bowling today.

In bowling alley slang, a *turkey* is 3 strikes in a row. The term dates back to the late 1800s when, around the holidays, bowling

alley owners presented live turkeys to the first member of the team to score 3 consecutive strikes.

> A bowling pin needs to tilt only 7½ degrees to fall.

An adult human head weighs about 12 pounds (5.4 kilograms), or the same as a light bowling ball.

> In ancient Germany, *Heidenwerfen* was the popular word for bowling. It means "strike down the heathens."
> Short of 300, the highest recorded bowling score was not 299—it was 299½! In 1905, a player bowled his last ball in what would otherwise have been a perfect game. On impact, nine pins were instantly knocked down but a single pin split in half; the top part fell over, but the bottom remained standing.

Kicking Bass!

Thirty million Americans fish for bass every year, making it one of the top sports in the nation. One out of every 400 Americans (meaning 600,000 Americans), is a proud member of B.A.S.S., the Bass Anglers Sportsman Society. The average amateur fisherman spends about $200 a month on equipment, which adds up to a $40 billion industry.

Course 493: **Lap This Up!**

> A girl or woman swimmer can be called a *naiad*.
> On August 6, 1926, Gertrude Ederle, who was still a teenager, became the first woman to swim the English Channel. Not only did she swim the channel, but she broke the speed record held by a man.
> Pianist Yanni was formally a member of the Greek National Swimming Team.
> MGM film bathing beauty and box-office darling Esther Williams was a great swimmer who had qualified for three events in the 1940 Olympics, only to have them preempted by World War II.
> Kim Basinger's mother was a champion swimmer who performed water ballets in several Esther Williams movies in the 1940s.
> To a competitive swimmer, "d.p.s." means distance per stroke.

Swimming pools in the United States contain enough water to cover the city of San Francisco with a layer of water about 7 feet deep. Another major quake could also produce the same result.

Divorced from Reality?

Persons who engage in solitary endurance sports are the ones most likely to be compulsive exercisers—i.e., joggers, long-distance swimmers, weight lifters, and cross-country skiers. Frequently, devotees of these activities set unrealistic, ambitious goals and then drive themselves mercilessly to reach them. A study of New York marathoners a few years ago found that their divorce rate—both male and female—was twice the national average.

Watch Out, You Guys . . .

Nearly 1 million women in the United States take their rifles and go hunting annually. Hopefully, they aren't hunting for a date!

Course 489: Going for the Gold

> As of 2000, the country of Nepal had never won an Olympic medal.
> The field hockey event is the only event in which India has ever won any gold medals at the Olympics.
> Cleveland Stadium was built for what became a failed attempt by the city to host the 1932 Olympic Games.

Of the 192 countries on Earth, 3 of them—Kiribati, Marshall Islands, and Vatican City—have no National Olympic Committees.

> Debi Thomas was the first black athlete to win a medal at the Winter Olympics, and is the holder of 2 national championships and 1 world title in figure skating. She is now an aspiring orthopedic surgeon at Chicago's Northwestern University Medical School.
> The first female athlete to appear in a Wheaties "Breakfast of Champions" television commercial was Mary Lou Retton, shortly after her gold medal win at the 1984 Summer Olympics.
> The largest Olympic stadium ever constructed was Stadium Australia in Olympic Park. It seats 110,000 people. Opening and closing ceremonies, men's soccer finals, and athletic events were held there.

To produce handles for the 10,000 Olympic torches carried in the 15,000 mile U.S. relay for the 1996 Summer Olympics, 60 pecan trees were used.

> Up to 20,000 pounds of pressure per square inch may be absorbed by a pole-vaulter on the joints of his tubular thigh bones when he lands.
> No high jumper has ever been able to stay off the ground for more than one second.
> Mark Spitz holds the all-time Olympic record for men's swimming events. At two Olympics (1968 and 1972), Spitz won a total of 11 medals.

A. C. Gilbert, the inventor of the Erector set, won an Olympic gold medal in 1908 for the pole vault.

> Montreal's Olympic Stadium was originally supposed to cost $120 million, but flawed workmanship and poor design, among other serious problems, will cause the price to mushroom to about $3 billion by the time the stadium is paid off in 2006.
> Discuss and hammer throwers are allowed only 2 spikes on each shoe.

The motto of the Olympics is "Citius, altius, fortius" which means "Faster, higher, stronger." But it sounds more like the motto for Viagra.

Man on the Run

Roger Bannister was the first man to break the 4-minute mile; however, he did not break the 4-minute mile in an actual race. On May 6, 1954, he ran 3:59.4, while being carefully paced by other runners. Bannister's quarter-mile splits were 57.5 seconds, 60.7, 62.3, and 58.9.

But 23 days after Bannister had run the most famous mile of all time, fellow Briton Diane Leather became the first woman to break 5 minutes with a time of 4:59.6 in Birmingham, England, on May 29, 1954. In the 40-plus years since the two British runners broke these significant marks, women's times have improved by a far higher percentage than men's.

Final Exam

1. The most popular sport in American nudist camps is softball.

True or False?

2. The ancient Greeks awarded cabbages to winners of sports events, and they were often carried by marathon runners.

True or False?

3. It is believed that the slang phrase "give me a break" originated as a pool hall expression.

True or False?

4. A forfeited baseball game is recorded as 1–0.

True or False?

5. Pittsburgh is the only city where all the major sports teams have the same owner.

True or False?

6. Soccer gave us the term *melee*.

True or False?

7. The pitcher who has totalled up more victories than anyone else in Major League history but never won the prestigious Cy Young Award was Sandy Koufax.

True or False?

8. The California Academy of Tauromaquia in San Diego is a world-renowned school for soccer players.

True or False?

9. The depression made in the snow by a skier who has fallen backward is called a *sitzmark*.

True or False?

10. The sport of sailing usually has a racecourse in the shape of a rectangle.

True or False?

ANSWERS

1. FALSE. It's volleyball, but please watch those spikes!

2. FALSE. They were awarded celery.

3. TRUE.

4. FALSE. It is recorded as nine-to-nothing.

5. FALSE. All the teams have the same colors: black and gold.

6. TRUE. It means a "confused mass," which was what the playing field looked like in Europe in the Middle Ages. Towns competed using teams of up to a hundred players, with the goals set a half-mile or so apart.

7. FALSE. It was Cy Young, of course!

8. FALSE. It is a school for matadors.

9. TRUE.

10. FALSE. The racecourse is in the shape of a triangle.

6

The USELESS
School of
Science
and Technology

Next time someone asks you for a couple of aspirin, give him a real headache. As he's swallowing the pills, mention the fact that the Bayer company, developer of that painkiller, also invented heroin in the early 1900s—and trademarked the name. It was initially prescribed as a cough suppressant and a cure for addiction to morphine and codeine, but was recognized as a dangerously addictive substance by 1905. That should provoke some useless conversations about the drug problem in America.

Meanwhile, if you're chattering on the phone, and there's a lack of intelligent conversation, you can always mention that the inventor of the telephone—Alexander Graham Bell—had the odd habit of drinking his soup through a glass straw. On another technical note, should someone be extolling the virtues of their new personal computer or of Bill Gates, counter his train of thought with your own hero—Herman Hollerith. Who? Well, it just so happens Herman used a computerlike device named the Hollerith Tabulator to take the U.S. Census in 1890, long before even the first official computer UNIVAC came into existence.

But don't stop there. Ask your next victims about Albert Einstein, and naturally they'll identify him as the brains behind the Theory of Relativity, etc., etc. However, they probably don't know that he was also offered the job of first president of the State of Israel, which he turned down. Luckily, Louis-Jacques-Mandé Daguerre, the developer of modern photography, didn't turn down an annual pension of 6,000 francs from the French government in exchange for the secret of his photographic process. Otherwise, your family photos might just be crayon drawings. By the way, if you'd like to take a photo of Einstein's brain, it's located in New Jersey.

For laughs, humiliate someone who claims to know everything about the stars. Just ask him if any deaths have been caused by a meteor. When he gets that glassy stare, inform him that a dog was killed by a hurtling space rock at Nakhla, Egypt, in 1911. What's more, the unlucky canine is the only creature known to have been killed by a meteor.

Clearly, when it comes to USELESS KNOWLEDGE, we've done quite a bit of scientific research. Now it's your turn!

Course 501: **Handy Household Items**

> As World War I raged through Europe in 1917, Ed Cox of San Francisco invented a presoaped pad with which to clean pots. His wife named it S.O.S., which, as the story goes, stood for "Save Our Saucepans."
> Chester Greenwood from the United States was 15 years old in 1873 when he invented earmuffs.
> In 1946, Marion Donovan was surprised when her prototype for disposable paper diapers was met with ridicule. She journeyed to all the major U.S. paper companies, and was laughed at for proposing such an "unnecessary

and impractical" item to replace cotton diapers. After nearly 10 years of pitching her revolutionary idea, Victor Mills had the foresight to capitalize on it, and he became the creator of Pampers.

> The monkey wrench is named after its inventor, a London blacksmith named Charles Moncke.

The fishbowl was invented in the middle of the eighteenth century by Countess Du Barry, mistress of France's King Louis XV.

> The Chinese invented eyeglasses. Marco Polo reported seeing many pairs worn by the Chinese as early as 1275—500 years before lens grinding became an art in the West.
> In 1832, Scottish surgeon Neil Arnott devised water beds to improve his patients' comfort.
> Sure, Leonardo da Vinci painted the *Mona Lisa*, but even more important, he invented the scissors.
> Leonardo da Vinci wrote notebook entries in mirror (backwards) script, a trick that kept many of his observations from being widely known until decades after his death.

M. R. Bissell had a china shop in Grand Rapids, Michigan, and was allergic to the dusty straw scattered on the floor after unpacking china from crates. So, he invented the first carpet sweeper in 1876 to clean up the mess and protect his sinuses.

> Lillian Moller Gilbreth (1878–1972), the mother of 12 children, patented many devices, including an electric food mixer and the trash can with step-on lid-opener that can be found in most households today.
> Early handheld lights used carbon-zinc batteries that did not last very long. To keep the light burning required that the user turn it on for a short time and then turn it off to allow the battery to recover. That's how they originally became known as a flashlight.
> At the turn of the century, most lightbulbs were handblown, and the cost of one was equivalent to half a day's pay for the average U.S. worker.
> The modern zipper, the talon slide fastener, was invented in 1913 but didn't catch on until the first dresses incorporating it appeared in the 1930s.

Camel's-hair brushes are not made of camel's hair. They were invented by a man named Camel.

> Miami Beach pharmacist Benjamin Green invented the first suntan lotion by cooking cocoa butter in a granite coffeepot on his wife's stove, and then testing the batch on his own head. His invention was introduced as Coppertone Suntan Cream in 1944.

> In the early 1940s, Swiss inventor George de Mestral took a walk with his dog. Upon returning home, he noticed that his pants were covered with cockleburrs. His studied them under a microscope, where he discovered their natural hooklike shape. This became the basis for a unique, two-sided fastener: one side with stiff "hooks" like the burrs and the other side with the soft "loops" like the fabric of his pants. The result was VELCRO® brand fasteners, named for the French words *velour* and *crochet*.

> A device invented as a primitive steam engine by the Greek engineer Hero more than 2,000 years ago is used today as a rotating lawn sprinkler.

> Air-conditioning was invented by Willis Carrier to help a Brooklyn, New York, printer get decent color during hot, humid weather. Air-conditioning wasn't used for cooling people until 1924, when it made its debut at the J. L. Hudson Department Store in Detroit, Michigan.

Levi Hutchins of Concord, New Hampshire, invented the first alarm clock in 1787. It only rang at 4 A.M. because that's what time he got up.

> Edwin Land, inventor of the Polaroid camera, is second only to Thomas Edison in the number of U.S. patents granted him for inventions.

> Arch supports were created by Konrad Birkenstock in 1897. He designed shoes that followed the shape of the foot so that comfort would increase. The basic design revolutionized the footwear industry.

> The invention of typing correction fluid is credited to the mother of former Monkee Mike Nesmith. She named the product Liquid Paper, and in 1979 she sold the rights to the Gillette Company for millions.

In 1875, the director of the U.S. Patent Office sent in his resignation and advised that his department be closed. There was nothing left to invent, he claimed.

Course 509: In the Bathroom

> In 1840, poet Henry Wadsworth Longfellow became the first American to have plumbing installed in his house.

> Shampoo was first marketed in the United States in 1930 by John Breck, who was the captain of a volunteer fire department.

> The Chinese are credited with inventing the first toothbrushes in the late 1400s. The bristles were made of hog bristles, which were highly effective and popular. Later, when nylon was invented, it replaced them.

The biography of Thomas Crapper, the British sanitary engineer who invented the modern flush toilet in 1878, was called *Flushed with Pride: The Story of Thomas Crapper.*

> Ivory Soap was originally named P&G White Soap. In 1879, Harley Proctor found the new name during a reading in church of the 45th Psalm: "All thy garments smell of myrrh, and aloes, and cassia, out of ivory palaces, whereby they have made thee glad."
> In 1881, Procter & Gamble's Harley Procter decided that adding the word "pure" to the packaging of his Ivory soap would give its sales a necessary shot in the arm. Analysis proved that Ivory was almost 100 percent pure fatty acids and alkali—the stuff that most soap is made of anyway. So Harley marked his soap "99 and $^{44}/_{100}$ percent pure," deciding that using the exact number sounded more credible than rounding up to 100 percent.
> In 1857, Joseph C. Gayetty of New York City invented toilet paper.

Before bath tissue was introduced in the United States in perforated form in 1884, a number of outhouses in America were stocked with dried leaves.

> KLEENEX® Cleansing Tissues were invented in 1924 as a sanitary way to remove cold cream.
> Colgate was the first toothpaste sold in metal tubes rather than jars.
> The average life expectancy of a toilet is 50 years.

Course 517: **Let's Get Digital**

> In 1843, mathematician Ada Byron published the first computer programs based on a punched-card idea. They were for the general-purpose mechanical digital computer, which had just been invented by Charles Babbage.
> In 1886, Herman Hollerith had the idea of using punched cards to keep and transport information, a technology used up to the late 1970s. This device was originally constructed to allow the 1890 census to be tabulated. The Tabulating Machine Company was founded by him in the same year. Twenty-eight years later, after several takeovers, the company founded by Hollerith became known as International Business Machines (IBM).

Before Rudy Giuliani in 2001, *Time* magazine named the computer "Man of the Year" in 1982.

> A 1999 survey of 25,500 standard English-language dictionary words found that 93 percent of them have been registered as dot-coms.
> Because the eyes work harder when viewing objects up close, it is the proximity of the computer monitor to the eyes that causes eyestrain, not "radiation"

emitted from the screen. According to the American Academy of Ophthalmology, using a video display terminal will not harm your eyes.

> In 1952, CBS made computer history by being the first to use a computer, the UNIVAC I, to forecast the U.S. presidential election.

During the height of the Y2K panic in 1999, the U.S. Federal Reserve released $200 billion to defend American banks from a mass cash withdrawal spurred by apocalyptic terror of computer crashes.

> ENIAC, the first electronic computer, appeared 50 years ago. The original ENIAC was about 80 feet long, weighed 30 tons, had 17,000 tubes. By comparison, a desktop computer today can store a million times more information than an ENIAC, and is 50,000 times faster.

> A chip of silicon a quarter-inch square has the capacity of the original 1949 ENIAC computer, which occupied a full city block.

> From the smallest microprocessor to the biggest mainframe, the average American depends on more than 264 computers per day.

It was recently reported that the technology contained in a single Game Boy unit in 2000 exceeded all the computer power that was used to put the first man on the Moon.

> Laptop computers falling from the overhead bins onto passengers' heads are among the most common accidents aboard airplanes.

> Nearly 60 percent of women say they receive at least eleven e-mails a day, while only 49 percent of men say they do.

> The first domain name ever registered was *Symbolics.com*. The domain name was registered on March 15, 1985, by Symbolics Technology, Inc.

In Web site addresses on the Internet, "http" stands for "hypertext transfer protocol."

> The Vatican's Web site is powered by three host computers named after archangels—Raphael, Michael, and Gabriel.

There are hefty price tags on some Internet domain names. The highest-selling domain name to date, *business.com*, went for $7.5 million in 1999. The buyer was eCompanies.

> You can't use a U.S. computer monitor in Australia because the colors would be wrong. The magnetic field of the Earth pulls the electron beams hitting the cathode tube to a position relative to its position in the magnetic field.

> With U.S. trademark No. 2,347,676, the sad emoticon ":-(" gets the same protection as a corporate logo or any similar intellectual property. Although

seen on millions of e-mails, the mark is now officially owned by Despair—a "de-motivational" company that sells humorous posters about futility, failure, and depression to "pessimists, losers, and underachievers."

Elwood Edwards's voice is heard more than 27 million times a day (which comes to more than 18,000 times per minute). Edwards is the man behind those special three words—no, not "I love you," but "You've got mail."

THE HISTORY OF FIVE "NERDS"

1. The first technology corporation to move into California's Silicon Valley was Hewlett-Packard, in 1938. Stanford University engineers Bill Hewlett and Dave Packard started their company in a Palo Alto garage with $1,538. Their first product was an audio oscillator bought by Walt Disney Studios for use in the making of *Fantasia*.

2. Apple cofounder Steve Wozniak earned money in college by selling "blue boxes" to other students. A blue box attached to a pay phone created the proper signals to allow a user to make free phone calls.

3. Microsoft CEO Bill Gates formed a company to sell a computerized traffic counting system to cities, which made $20,000 its first year. Business dropped sharply when customers learned that Gates was only 14 years old.

4. In October 1994, Jeff Bezos wanted to name his new Web venture "Cadabra," as in "abracadabra." But his attorney convinced him that this magical moniker sounded a bit too much like "cadaver." Reluctantly, Bezos went with his second choice: *Amazon.com*.

5. Peter de Jager was the world's foremost expert on the Y2K problem, which many believed would cause computer systems to collapse because their software would mistake the double zeroes of 2000 to mean 1900. He wrote the "Doomsday 2000" article that initially publicized the problem, then spent the 1990s helping companies all over the world fix their computers. When at midnight, January 1, 2000, planes did not fall from the sky, de Jager was angrily accused of setting the hysterical stage for billions of dollars to be wasted.

Course 525: **Toy Stories**

> The classic toy wagon was designed by Antonio Pasin, who founded his company in 1918. Pasin wanted to give his wagons a modern flair, and chose the word "radio" for what was then a new form of communication, and "flyer" for the wonder of flight—hence, "Radio Flyer."

> Artist Xavier Roberts first designed his soon-to-be-famous Cabbage Patch dolls in 1977 to help pay his way through school. They had soft faces and were made by hand, as opposed to the hard-faced mass-market dolls, and were originally called Little People.

> Barbie® and Ken® Dolls are named after Mattel founders Ruth and Elliot Handler's son and daughter, Barbara and Ken. Barbie's® full name is Barbie Millicent Roberts, and she is from Willows, Wisconsin. First sold in 1959, Barbie® wasn't given bendable legs until 1965.

Mark Twain invented a board game similar to Trivial Pursuit. He called it Mark Twain's Memory-Builder.

> In 1914, Charles Pajeau hired midgets, dressed them in elf costumes, and had them play with his new invention, Tinker Toys, in the window of a Chicago store during Christmas. This publicity stunt made the construction toy an instant hit. A year later, over a million sets had been sold.

> In 1966, Elliot Handler, one of the cofounders of Mattel, was also the inventor of Hot Wheels®. The innovative gravity-powered car had special low-friction styrene wheels. Tiny Hot Wheels® vehicles have been clocked at speeds of up to 300 miles per hour.

> Silly Putty started as a mistake in a New Haven laboratory, and was turned into a consumer hit in the 1960s. According to engineers, Silly Putty is a self-contradiction. Chemically, it is a liquid, but it resembles a solid. The molecular structure will stretch if the structure is slowly pulled. But if tugged, it snaps apart. The toy has a rebound capacity of 75 to 80 percent, whereas a rubber ball has only about 50-percent capacity. A silicon derivative, Silly Putty won't rot; it can withstand temperatures from minus 70° Fahrenheit to hundreds of degrees above zero. On top of all that, it picks up newsprint, which often appears sharper than the original.

A ball of glass will bounce higher than a ball of rubber. A ball of solid steel will bounce higher than one made entirely of glass.

> Spacewar is generally considered to be the first video game. Programmed in 1962 by MIT student Steve Russell, it was a simple game in which two players would blast lasers at each other. At the time, the game only ran on massive, million-dollar mainframes the size of a small house. Spacewar was circulated to other computer labs across the country, but only nerdy college students with access to mainframes could play it.

> The popular drawing toy Etch a Sketch, invented by Arthur Granjean, was originally named the L'Ecran Magique. Sales skyrocketed in 1960 after its name changed and some innovative TV advertising was launched.

Emerson Moser, once Crayola's senior crayon maker, revealed upon his retirement that he was blue-green colorblind and couldn't see all the Crayola colors. He molded more than 1.4 billion crayons in his 37-year career.

> The only change in the original design of Slinky since its launch in 1945 has been to crimp the ends as a safety measure.
> Slinky has gone in space shuttles to test zero-gravity on the physical laws that govern the mechanics of springs. In space, Slinky behaves like neither a spring nor a toy, but as a continuously propagating wave.
> The man behind the Beanie Babies phenomenon of the late 1990s is still quite a mystery. Ty Warner has shunned interviews, and the company's financial records and phone number are hard to find. Reports in 1999 identified Warner as a billionaire and the richest toy maker in the world. He purchased New York's Four Seasons luxury hotel for $275 million.

The revolutionary Pac Man video arcade game featured colored ghosts named Inky, Blinky, Pinky, and Clyde.

WHAT A BALL!

The Super Ball® was born in 1965, and it became America's most popular plaything that year. By Christmas time, only six months after Super Balls were introduced by Wham-O, 7 million balls had been sold at 98 cents apiece.

Norman Stingley, a California chemist, invented the remarkable bouncing gray ball. He had compressed a synthetic rubber material under 3,500 pounds of pressure per square inch. It had a resiliency of 92 percent, about three times that of a tennis ball, and could bounce for long periods.

It was reported that presidential aide McGeorge Bundy had five dozen Super Balls® shipped to the White House for the amusement of staffers.

Course 532: **Boys Under the Hood**

> Albert Einstein never learned how to drive a car.
> Henry Ford called his first car a quadricycle, but he did not invent the automobile. What Ford did accomplish was to mass-produce automobiles and provide affordable service for them.

Karl Benz of Germany is credited with inventing the very first automobile in 1885. It had an internal combustion engine and three wheels. In 1926, Benz merged his company with that of fellow German auto creator Gustave Daimler to form Mercedes-Benz.

> The driver's test was invented in France. In 1893, drivers of all self-propelled vehicles had to undergo an exam that tested driving and vehicle-repair ability.
> Donald F. Duncan, the man who made the yo-yo an American tradition, is also credited with popularizing the parking meter (yeah, thanks).
> In 1899, the Belgian Jenatzy became the first driver to reach a speed of over 100 kilometers per hour. He was driving his electrically powered car *La Jamais Contente*.

Ferdinand Porsche, who later went on to build the famous sports cars bearing his own name, designed the original 1936 Volkswagen.

> The British Council of Manufacturers publicly claimed in 1948 that the Volkswagen Beetle would be "popular for two to three years."
> As an advertising gimmick, Carl Mayer, nephew of lunch-meat mogul Oscar Mayer, invented the company's "Wienermobile." On July 18, 1936, the first Oscar Mayer® Wienermobile rolled out of General Body Company's factory in Chicago. Wienermobiles still tour the United States today.
> The power lawn mower was invented by Ransom E. Olds (of Oldsmobile fame) in 1915.

The world's first electric traffic light signal was installed 75 years ago in Cleveland, Ohio, at the intersection of Euclid Avenue and East 105th St.

> Cooking and salad oils could lubricate machinery, such as cars and boats, according to Penn State chemical engineers. Tests found that when blended with an additive developed at Penn State, some vegetable oils perform as well as or better than commercial oils.
> On September 13, 1913, the famous Lincoln Highway, the first paved trans-American highway, was completed, running from New York to San Francisco. In 1928, thousands of Boy Scouts fanned out along the highway. At an average of about one per mile, they installed concrete markers with a small bust of Lincoln, dedicating the road to his memory.
> The initials "M. G." on the famous British-made automobile stand for Morris Garage.
> Why isn't the Chevy Nova sold in South America? *No va* means "it doesn't go" in Spanish!

U.S. Patent No. D219,584 was issued in 1970 to veteran movie actor Steve McQueen. He was famous not only for his movies but also for racing cars and working on engines. A by-product of his racing hobby was the invention of the bucket seat.

Course 547: **War News**

> At the outset of the Manhattan Project, Albert Einstein was one of the scientists who forecast that an A-bomb would have to be so large and heavy that it would require a ship to deliver it to its target.
> The historic notebooks in which Marie and Pierre Curie recorded their experiments on radium, nearly a century ago, are still radioactive.
> On August 22, 1849, Austria launched unmanned balloons carrying bombs with time-delay fuses against Venice. It was the first use of aircraft in warfare.

Britain developed the first tanks for use during World War I. The word *tank* was used because it didn't mean anything, and didn't give the Germans a clue as to the weapon's possible use.

> While fighting with the French underground during World War II, Jacques Yves Cousteau invented the aqualung, the self-contained device that supplies air pressure for underwater divers.
> An ordinary TNT bomb involves atomic reaction, and could be called an atomic bomb. What we call an A-bomb involves nuclear reactions and should be called a nuclear bomb.
> On July 11, 1946, Micheline Bernardini of Paris modeled for the first photograph of a bikini. The tiny swimsuit was named after Bikini Atoll in the Marshall Islands, the site of atomic testing ten days earlier.

In 1969, the navy spent $375,000 on an "aerodynamic analysis of the self-suspended flare." The study's conclusion was that the Frisbee was not feasible as military hardware.

Course 550: **Getting off the Ground**

> J. P. Blanchard, a Frenchman, is credited with having been the first person to use a parachute. In 1785, from a balloon high in the air, he dropped a dog in a basket to which a parachute was attached. Blanchard also claimed to have descended from a balloon in a parachute in 1793.
> Dr. Samuel Langley was able to get many model airplanes to fly, but on December 8, 1903, Langley's "human-carrying flying machine," the aerodrome, plunged into the Potomac River near Washington, D.C., in front of photographers assembled to witness his flight. Reporters around the country made fun of the idea that people could fly—but nine days later, Wilbur and Orville Wright proved them wrong.
> The first person killed in an airplane accident was Lt. Thomas E. Selfridge. On September 17, 1908, Selfridge was a passenger with Orville Wright in a

demonstration flight at Fort Myer, Virginia, when the crash occurred. Wright survived. The first pilot of a powered airplane to be killed was Eugène Lefèbvre, in France on September 7, 1909.

The first commercial passenger airplane began flying in 1914. The first commercial passenger airplane with a bathroom began flying in 1919.

> When airplanes were still a novel invention, seat belts for pilots were installed only after the consequence of their absence was observed to be fatal—several pilots fell to their deaths while flying upside down inside the cockpit.
> Charles Lindbergh was not the first man to cross the Atlantic in an aircraft; he was the 67th. The first 66 made the crossing in dirigibles and twin-engine mail planes. Lindbergh was the first to make the dangerous flight by himself.
> The first jet passenger airliner was the de Havilland Comet, which serviced the British Overseas Airways, starting in May of 1952.

Lockheed, manufacturer of the Trident missile, transmits data from its Sunnyvale, California, headquarters to its plant 30 miles away in Santa Cruz via carrier pigeon.

> In the airplane known as the DC-10, the letters "DC" stand for Douglas Commercial.

The first human-made object to break the sound barrier was a whip. As the energy increases from the handle to the end of the whip, the energy is moving beyond the speed of sound at the tip. That's why a whip makes such a loud cracking noise.

> Only 16 Concordes were ever made, the last in 1980. On New Year's Eve 1994, one Concorde plane carried wealthy revelers on a 32-hour trip to nowhere. These travelers, who paid $23,000 apiece for the trip, rang in the New Year twice because they crossed the International Date Line.
> The B-2 Stealth Bomber is designed to fly undetected by radar. However, it has been known to show as visible on radar systems when it was wet or when the humidity was high. It is also susceptible when the bomb bay is open just before delivering a bomb.

An airplane's black box recorder actually isn't black but orange.

> The Boeing 767 aircraft is a collection of 3.1 million parts from 800 different suppliers around the world: fuselage parts from Japan, center wing section from Southern California, and flaps from Italy.
> The wingspan of a Boeing 747 jet is longer than the length of the Wright Brothers' first flight.

> Australia's airline, Qantas, was formed in 1920. Its name came from the initials of Queensland and Northern Territory Air Services, not—as some may have suspected—from a native species of bird or marsupial.

Built in 1967, the world's only flying saucer launching pad is in St. Paul, Alberta, Canada.

Perfect for Sticky Situations

In 1938 DuPont scientist Dr. Roy Plunkett accidentally created Teflon, but his company wasn't excited about it. As DuPont dragged its heels, a Parisian named Marc Gregoire learned of Teflon, and at his wife's urging managed to apply it to her pots and pans. Within several years, this entrepreneur sold in excess of 1 million pieces of Tefal (his name for Teflon) cookware.

But the concept of Teflon did not stick in America. When UPI reporter Thomas Hardie encountered one of these coated pans in France, he saw a niche in the domestic market and contacted Marc Gregoire. Hardie then pitched the product to every major U.S. manufacturer of cooking utensils, but to no avail.

Finally, he convinced a buyer at Macy's to take 200 pans off his hands. All sold within two days, despite a major snowstorm. But Hardie could not keep up with the demand. While he was building a plant to produce his product, other companies seized the opportunity and forged their own coated cookware.

Course 563: **Got Hang-ups?**

> Alexander Graham Bell applied for his patent on the telephone, an "Improvement in Telegraphy," on Valentine's Day, 1876.
> Alexander Graham Bell, inventor of the telephone, was originally an instructor of deaf children and invented the telephone to help his deaf wife and mother to hear.
> In 1889, the first coin-operated telephone, patented by Connecticut inventor William Gray, was installed in Hartford. Soon, pay phones were installed in stores, hotels, saloons, and restaurants, and their use soared. Local calls using a coin-operated phone in the United States cost only 5 cents everywhere until 1951.

When commercial telephone service was introduced between New York and London in 1927, the first three minutes of a call cost $75.00.

- When using the first pay telephones, a caller did not deposit coins in the machine. He or she gave them to an attendant who stood next to the telephone. Self-service coin telephones did not appear until 1899.
- The first operators employed by the Bell Telephone Company were young boys who worked standing up. Only after several years did it occur to anybody to provide them with chairs.
- The first female operator was Emma M. Nutt, who started working for the Telephone Dispatch Company in Boston on September 1, 1878.
- Coast-to-coast direct-dial telephone service became available in the United States on November 10, 1951.

In Saudi Arabia there are solar-powered pay phones in the desert.

- The first telephone book ever issued contained only 50 names. It was published in New Haven, Connecticut, by the New Haven District Telephone Company in February 1878.
- In 1970, MCI stood for Microwave Communications, Inc. No longer used as an acronym, it now stands alone.
- Not until Herbert Hoover became U.S. president in 1929 did the U.S. chief executive have a private telephone in his office. The booth in a White House hallway had served as the president's private phone before one was installed in the Oval Office.

The telephone area code for a cruise ship crossing the Atlantic Ocean is 871.

Course 574: **What's Up, Doc?**

- The most advanced area of medicine in the ancient world was ophthalmic surgery. Celsus (A.D. 14–37) left detailed descriptions of delicate cataract surgery using sophisticated needle syringes.
- John Greenwood invented the dental drill in 1790.
- The modern hypodermic needle was invented in 1853. It was initially used for giving injections of morphine as a painkiller. Physicians mistakenly believed that morphine would not be addictive if it bypassed the digestive tract.

In the mid 1880s, until about 1910, undertakers sold Grave Alarm devices. These were elaborate rope-and-bell/pulley arrangements allowing those buried alive to summon help. The rope was placed into the hand of the (supposed) deceased, and it wound through a series of tubes to the bell outside the grave.

> Until recent years, people living in remote areas of Afghanistan and
> Ethiopia were immunized against smallpox by having dried powdered
> scabs from victims of the disease blown up their noses. This treatment
> was invented by a Chinese Buddhist nun in the eleventh century. It is the
> oldest known form of vaccination.
> Paul Winchell, the ventriloquist, was not only the voice of Jerry Mahoney,
> Knucklehead, and Tigger in the Winnie the Pooh films, he also invented the
> artificial heart. He donated the patent for it to the University of Utah.

**Hospitals make money by selling the umbilical cords cut from
women who have given birth. The cords are reused in vein-
transplant surgery.**

> In 1953, Catherine and Carolyn Mouton became the first Siamese twins
> successfully separated by surgery.
> Penicillin causes about 300 deaths in the United States every year.

BAYER'S HEADACHE

In 1897, building on earlier research, a chemist from the Bayer Company in
Germany, Felix Hoffman, invented a recipe to help relieve the painful symptoms of
his father's arthritis. He then pitched his idea to his employer, and Bayer reluctantly
agreed to produce the medicine they named Aspirin.

Bayer finally launched Aspirin in 1915. But Aspirin's success ended up costing
the company a great deal of money in 1919, when the United States, England, France,
and Italy forced Bayer to surrender the trademark to them as part of the Treaty of
Versailles. Thus the word *aspirin* is now written in the lower case.

**Oh yes, Bayer also held, and was forced to give up, its trade-
mark to Heroin at the end of World War I as well.**

Course 586: **The First**

> The first person to work out the use of fingerprints for identification purposes,
> English anthropologist Francis Galton, was a first cousin of Charles Darwin.
> The first ballpoint pens, sold in 1945, were priced at $12.00 apiece.
> The first Band-Aid Brand Adhesive Bandages were 3 inches wide and
> 18 inches long. You made your own bandage by cutting off as much as
> you needed.
> The first coin-operated machine ever designed was a holy-water dispenser
> that required a 5-drachma piece to operate. It was the brainchild of the Greek
> scientist Hero in the first century A.D.

The first commercial vacuum cleaner was so large that it was mounted on a wagon. People threw parties in their homes so guests could watch the new device do its job.

> The first drive-in service station in the United States was opened by Gulf Oil Company on December 1, 1913, in Pittsburgh, Pennsylvania.
> The first hot-air balloon to carry passengers was invented by the Montgolfier brothers in France in 1783. It flew 5 miles.
> The first lighthouse to use electricity was the Statue of Liberty in 1886.

The first envelopes with gummed flaps were produced in 1844. In Great Britain, they were not immediately popular because it was thought to be a serious insult to send a person's saliva to someone else.

> *The Adventures of Tom Sawyer,* by Mark Twain, was the first published novel ever to have been written on a typewriter.
> The first practical can opener was developed many years after the birth of the metal can. Early cans were made of iron and weighed more than the food they held. Ezra Warner of Waterbury, Connecticut patented the first can opener in 1858, but it never left the grocery store. A clerk had to open each can before it was taken away. William Lyman of the United States invented the modern can opener, with a cutting wheel that rolls around the rim, in 1870.
> The first product to have a UPC bar code on its packaging was Wrigley's chewing gum.

The first sewing machine was patented in 1846, by Elias Howe. It didn't catch on, and in 1851 the now-broke Howe sold the patent to Isaac Singer for $2,000 in 1851. Hence, Singer Sewing Machines.

> The first rubber heel for shoes was patented on January 24, 1899 by Humphrey O'Sullivan. O'Sullivan, an Irish-American, found that his rubber heel outlasted the leather heel then in use.
> The first VCR, or videocassette recorder, was made in 1956 and was the size of a piano.
> Thomas Edison, the first person to conceive the electric light, had a collection of 5,000 birds.

While living in Memphis, Tennessee, in 1866–67, Thomas Edison developed the first device to electrocute cockroaches—and possibly, the last.

Course 589: **Creating Some Space**

> Aristarchus, a Greek astronomer living about 200 B.C., reportedly was the first person to declare that the Earth revolved around the sun. His theory was disregarded for hundreds of years.

In *Gulliver's Travels,* Jonathan Swift described the two moons of Mars, Phobos and Deimos, giving their exact size and speeds of rotation. He did this more than a hundred years before either moon was discovered.

> Galileo became totally blind shortly before his death, probably because of the damage done to his eyes during his many years of looking at the Sun through a telescope.

> After being forced by church officials to state in public that the earth does not rotate, Galileo is said to have muttered under his breath, "But it does move."

Proxima Centauri—not Alpha Centauri—is the closest star to Earth.

> A car traveling at a constant speed of 60 miles per hour would take more than 48 million years to reach the nearest star (other than our Sun), Proxima Centauri. This is about 685,000 average human lifetimes.

> A *pulsar* is a small star made up of neutrons so densely packed together that if one the size of a silver dollar landed on Earth, it would weigh approximately 100 million tons.

> A space vehicle must move at a rate of at least 17 miles per second to escape Earth's gravitational pull. This is equivalent to going from New York to Philadelphia in about 20 seconds.

> About 27 tons of dust rain down on Earth each day from space, making a total of almost 10,000 tons each year.

A sunbeam setting out through space at the rate of 186,000 miles a second would go in a gigantic circle and return to its origins after about 200 billion years.

> If Earth were the size and weight of a table tennis ball, the Sun would measure 12 feet and weigh 3 tons. On this scale, Earth would orbit the sun at a distance of 1,325 feet.

If a pin were heated to the same temperature as the center of the Sun, its fierce heat would set everything within 60 miles ablaze.

> If you attempted to count the stars in a galaxy at a rate of one every second,

it would take around 3,000 years to count them all.

> The energy released in one hour by just a single sunspot is equal to all the electrical power that will be used in the United States over the next million years.

Statistically speaking, UFO sightings are at their greatest number when Mars is closest to Earth.

> The famed U.S. Geological Survey astronomer, Dr. Shoemaker, wanted to be an astronaut but was rejected because of a medical problem. But after he died, his ashes were placed on board the *Lunar Prospector* spacecraft before NASA crashed the probe into a crater on July 31, 1999, to find out if there's water on the Moon—yes folks, your tax dollars at work!
> The size of the very first footprint on the Moon was 13 by 6 inches, the dimensions of Neil Armstrong's boot when he took his historic walk on July 20, 1969.

The footprints left by the Apollo astronauts will not erode since there is no wind or water on the Moon. They should last at least 10 million years.

> The surface of Venus—millions of miles away and hidden by clouds of sulphuric acid—has been better mapped than the Earth's seabed.
> When astronauts first shaved in space, their weightless whiskers floated up to the ceiling. A special razor had to be developed that drew the whiskers in like a vacuum cleaner.

Texas is the only state that permits residents to cast absentee ballots from space. The first to exercise this right to vote while in orbit was astronaut David Wolf, who cast his vote for Houston mayor via e-mail from the Russian space station *Mir* in November 1997.

SLIGHTLY OUT OF FOCUS

George Ellery Hale was the twentieth century's most important builder of telescopes. In 1897, Hale built a 40-inch-wide telescope, the largest ever built at that time. His second telescope, with a 60-inch lens, was set up in 1917 and took 14 years to build. During that time, Hale became convinced that he suffered from "Americanitis," a disorder in which the ambitions of Americans drive them insane. During the building of his lens, Hale spent time in a sanatorium, and would only discuss his plans for the telescope with a "sympathetic green elf."

Final Exam

1. The rickshaw was invented by the Chinese long before the Romans even had chariots.

True or False?

2. The creator of the Celsius scale—Anders Celsius—made freezing 0 degrees and boiling 100 degrees.

True or False?

3. Linus Pauling, who won a Nobel Prize for his research into vitamin C, also
discovered the cosmic "red shift," laying the foundation for the big bang theory.

True or False?

True or False?

4. The Soviet Union was the first country to send a woman into space.

True or False?

5. When the solar wind collides with the earth's magnetic field, we observe extremely high tides.

True or False?

6. George Washington Carver developed more unconventional products from clams than anyone else in history.

True or False?

7. James Ramsey invented a steam-driven motorboat in 1784. He ran it on the Potomac River, and the event was witnessed by George Washington.

True or False?

8. Most grandfather clocks with metal pendulums gain time in warm weather.

True or False?

9. The game of roulette was invented by the great French mathematician and philosopher Blaise Pascal. It was a by-product of his experiments with perpetual motion.

True or False?

10. Ants can survive being "nuked" in a microwave.

ANSWERS

1. FALSE. Rev. Jonathan Scobie, an American Baptist minister living in Yokohama, Japan, invented it. Reverend Scobie built the first model in 1869 in order to transport his invalid wife. Today the rickshaw remains a common mode of transportation in the Orient.

2. FALSE. He was an oddball scientist. When he first developed his scale, he made freezing one hundred degrees and boiling zero degrees. No one dared point out to him that this was upside down, so fellow scientists waited until Celsius died to change the scale to the one that most of the world uses today.

3. FALSE. It was Edwin Hubble—namesake of the Hubble telescope.

4. TRUE.

5. FALSE. The collision causes the aurora borealis.

6. FALSE. He created products including shaving cream, face cream, soap, and shampoo—all made from the lowly peanut.

7. TRUE.

8. FALSE. They lose time. This phenomenon occurs because most solids expand when heated. In the case of the clock, the higher temperature makes the metal pendulum longer, and thus slower.

9. TRUE.

10. TRUE. Microwave ovens have patterns of standing waves, with hot, very-high-density areas, and cold, very-low-density areas. Ants in the oven seek out the cold areas, and dodge the hot ones. If they run into a high-density area, they will survive, because their high surface-area-to-volume ratio cools them more quickly than the ratio of large objects, and buys them enough time to locate a cold spot.

7

The USELESS
School of
Music

Painstaking scientific research conducted over a period of several lunches revealed that 17,565,491,733,002 brain cells of a single hamster were imprinted with visions of Britney Spears's navel after it was forced to watch just five minutes of MTV. The implication is clear. Imagine how many of *your* precious brain cells have been subjected to similar damage. Of course, this isn't even taking into account all the neurons that have been neutralized by the Spice Girls, which would really be depressing.

But luckily for you, few areas of knowledge are as trivial as Useless Music Replacement Therapy. Next time the Beatles come up—like who was a better songwriter, Paul or John, blah, blah, blah—sidetrack the conversation with the fact that in *Magical Mystery Tour*, the rock group that opened for the Fab Four was the Bonzo Dog Band. Inevitably Neil Diamond will be mentioned. In that case, you can floor your companions with the news that not only did Neil write "Coming to America," but even more important, he penned the theme song for the television show *The Monkees*!

And since you'll be on a roll, why stop there!? When the subject of #1 songs gets injected into the conversation (and you can make sure it does), reveal that the only tune to hit the top spot twice on the charts in rock history was "The Twist," by Chubby Checker. But get even more obscure—ask your pals what was the first song played on Armed Forces Radio during Operation Desert Storm? Then answer your own question: "Rock the Casbah."

Finally, to leave them breathless, tell them you've always admired the rhythmic work of Jack Irons. Who? The drummer of the Red Hot Chili Peppers who was entered in *The Guinness Book of World Records* for playing the world's largest drum kit (308 pieces). That's right: you can forget Juilliard and those other high-class schools, because you'll never have a musical education more useless than this one!

Britney Spears's name is an anagram of "Presbyterians"!

Course 609: **Before the Music Played...**

> In 1960, before "Blowin' in the Wind," Bob Dylan was paid $50 for playing the harmonica on a Harry Belafonte album.
> Rod Stewart worked as a coffin polisher before his incredible recording career took off.
> Garth Brooks worked as a manager of a cowboy-boot store before he became the reigning male artist in country music.
> Before she became Rap royalty, Queen Latifah worked at Burger King.

Before becoming a worldwide icon, Madonna sold doughnuts at Dunkin' Donuts.

> Early in her career, Oscar-winning actress Angelina Jolie appeared in music videos of the Rolling Stones, Meatloaf, and Lenny Kravitz.

> Mariah Carey worked as a restaurant hostess before she hit it big as a singer.
> Before becoming hugely successful in her own right, singer Sheryl Crow sang backup vocals for Michael Jackson's 18-month *Bad* tour and later for Don Henley.
> Elvis Costello worked as a computer operator, at an Elizabeth Arden cosmetics factory.

Before the house in which the Menendez Brothers gunned down their parents became notorious, it had been rented by singer Prince, producer Hal Prince, and singer-pianist Elton John.

> Legendary musician and composer Frank Zappa was a greeting-card designer before he formed the Mothers of Invention.
> Between 1993 and 1996, Madonna lived in a 9-story-tall castle in Hollywood that once belonged to gangster Bugsy Siegel.

On February 17, 1964, the FBI launched a sweeping investigation into a problem that threatened to subvert the nation— namely, were the lyrics to the song "Louie Louie" by the Kingsmen filthy or not? After months of intensive analysis, the bureau was unable to conclude what the actual lyrics were, and the case was dropped. The tune, written by Richard Berry, remains the nation's most popular party song.

Freshman Music Quiz

1. The Trogs first performed "Wild Thing" and so did what other performer?

a) Jimi Hendrix
b) Jim Croce
c) Jim Morrison
d) Van Morrison

2. David Bowie could not use his real name because

a) Charles Manson ruined the name.
b) Davy Jones of the Monkees was popular first.
c) Elton John stole the name.
d) Davy Crockett was a hero who died at the Alamo.

3. For whom did Elton John write his 1975 hit song "Philadelphia Freedom"?

a) Ben Franklin
b) Wilson Goode
c) Billie Jean King
d) Jesse Jackson

4. How many Beatles songs did Elvis record?

a) 5
b) 4
c) 3
d) 0

5. The chart-topping pop group the Jackson Five was comprised of five brothers. Four of them were Jermaine, Michael, Tito, and Jackie. Who was the fifth?

a) Ben
b) Leon
c) Martin
d) Marlon

ANSWERS

1. a 2. b 3. c 4. a 5. d

The lead singer of the Knack, famous for the 1980s hit "My Sharona," and Dr. Jack Kevorkian's lead defense attorney are brothers: Doug and Jeffrey Feiger.

Course 619: **Don't Be Cruel**

> Elvis slept in the same bed with his mother, Gladys, until he reached puberty. Up until the time Elvis entered high school, she walked him back and forth to school every day and made him take along his own silverware so that he wouldn't catch germs from the other kids.

> Gladys also forbade young Elvis to go swimming or do anything that might put him in danger. What's more, the two of them conversed in a strange baby talk that only they could understand.

> Elvis Presley's hit recording of "Love Me Tender" entered *Billboard*'s pop charts in October 1956. The song, from Presley's debut film, was adapted from the tune "Aura Lee," which had been written back in 1861.

Elvis Presley wore a cross, a star of David, and the Hebrew letter *chi*. He explained his jewelry habit with, "I don't want to miss out on heaven due to a technicality."

> Supplied with individual headsets, tourists to Elvis Presley's Graceland mansion can listen to an audio tour presentation in a choice of languages: English, Spanish, Japanese, German, Italian, Dutch, French, and Portuguese.

> Elvis Presley made only one television commercial—an ad for "Southern Maid Doughnuts" that ran in 1954.

> *Rolling Stone* had an odd dilemma in 1994: the music journal had two fabulous photos of comedian Jerry Seinfeld impersonating Elvis Presley, but only one could go on the cover. To remedy this, the editors launched the magazine's first split cover. Half the issues featured Seinfeld as an old, puffy Elvis, and half featured him as a young, virile Elvis. The issues were sent randomly to subscribers in September 1994, and newsstands carried both versions.

Quentin Tarantino, the director of *Pulp Fiction,* appeared as an Elvis impersonator in an episode of the television sitcom *The Golden Girls.*

> Elvis Presley had two nicknames for his daughter, Lisa Marie Presley: Yisa and Buttonhead.

> Elvis treated his hair so harshly with dyes and styling products that, by the time he was forty, it had turned totally white.

> Elvis Presley's first Cadillac was blue before he bought it in 1955 and painted it pink.

> Elvis wanted to be a political activist, so he hand-delivered a letter to a White House guard and met with President Nixon on December 21, 1970. Presley embraced the president, gave him a gun, and stated that he had been studying "drug culture" for the last ten years. Nixon awarded Elvis an honorary Narcotics Bureau badge.

The most requested photo from the National Archives is a shot of Elvis shaking hands and offering his services as a drug-enforcement agent to Nixon.

> Elvis Presley died on August 16, 1977, at 42 years of age. An autopsy revealed more than 10 drugs in his system, including morphine and quaaludes.
> The legendary Groucho Marx died three days after Elvis Presley did. Unfortunately, due to all the fevered commotion caused by Presley's unanticipated death, the media paid little attention to the passing of this brilliant comedian and television, radio, and film star.

**"I don't know anything about music. In my line you don't have to."
—Elvis Presley**

THE KING AND I

In her 1985 autobiography, *Elvis and Me,* Priscilla Presley recalled the lack of dining etiquette of Elvis's buddies when she was his teenage bride: "Elvis's father, Vernon, resented the regulars acting as if Graceland was their personal club. They'd go into the kitchen at any hour and order anything they wanted. Naturally, everyone ordered something different. The cooks worked night and day keeping them happy. . . . What was really outrageous was that the regulars were ordering sirloin steaks or prime ribs while Elvis usually ate hamburgers or peanut butter and banana sandwiches. I wasn't too popular around Graceland when I started reorganizing the kitchen. I set down a policy of having one menu per meal, and anyone who didn't like what was on it could go to a local restaurant."

In August 1998, Priscilla Presley won $75,000 in a defamation lawsuit against Lavern Grant, a former army buddy of Elvis Presley's who claimed they had an affair before Priscilla married Presley. It was ruled in a California superior court that Grant made false statements that were repeated and used in the book *Child Bride: The Untold Story of Priscilla Beaulieu Presley* by Suzanne Finstad. Priscilla long assured the world she was a virgin when she married the King.

> Aerosmith liked to bring chainsaws with them on tour so that they could hack up hotel rooms more easily. They also traveled with extra-long extension cords, so that the televisions they tossed out windows would keep playing until they hit the ground.
> Aerosmith went berserk on their first Japanese tour. On opening night, they destroyed the backstage area when they found turkey roll on the buffet table. Lead singer Steven Tyler commented, "I explicitly said, 'No turkey roll.'"

After a concert, Van Halen's David Lee Roth would sit in the door of their tour bus and have the road manager douse his feet in Perrier.

> Declaring that he was an alcoholic, Ozzy Osbourne quit performing and opened a bar. He soon drank up all his stock and wasted his money until he rejoined his band.
> In 1978, Ted Nugent autographed a fan's arm by carving his name into the flesh with a bowie knife.
> Record label after record label signed the Sex Pistols then paid them to leave the label. In four months' time the recording industry paid the band £350,000 to go away.
> Smashing instruments became the Who's signature move. Each night they wrecked about £700 worth of equipment.

In a 1975 promotion, a fan won a date with Kiss's Gene Simmons. There was an embarrassing moment when Simmons had to take off his platform boots to fit in her Volkswagen.

> Rock and roll activist Ted Nugent drew heat in the summer of 2000 by saying that the Columbine tragedy could have been lessened if more concealed weapons were allowed in the United States.
> Motley Crue was kicked out of Germany in 1984. Their offense? Throwing mattresses out of hotel windows and watching them bounce off cars.

Nirvana front man Kurt Cobain once bought six turtles and put them in a bathtub in the middle of his living room. When the smell got too bad, he and a friend drilled a hole in the middle of the floor as a drain.

> When Neil Young arrived at Woodstock with Jimi Hendrix, they found they had to go several miles to reach the stage, so they stole a pickup truck and drove off. Later Young called the incident "one of the high points of my life."
> On a 1970 tour in San Francisco, California, Rod Stewart and fellow Faces members jumped on top of their rented station wagon and started jumping. When police arrived, the car had been crushed.

Baby Bust or Boom?

Hit tunes of the baby boomer era are being used (or overused) as advertising jingles. Here's just the tip of the iceberg:

Carly Simon's "Anticipation"—Heinz ketchup

Frank Sinatra's "My Way"—Kids' Cuisine

The Village People's "Macho Man"—Old El Paso

The Four Seasons' "Big Girls Don't Cry"—Johnson & Johnson hair detangler

The Temptations' "My Girl"—Sun Maid raisins

Roy Orbison's "Pretty Woman"—Tone Soap

The Beach Boys' "Fun, Fun, Fun"—Southwest Airlines

Gene Chandler's "Duke of Earl"—Best Foods Dijonaisse

Burger King earns the dubious award for using more old rock tunes in TV ads than any other U.S. company to sell its burgers.

Course 647: **Sing Along with Death**

> Alice Cooper liked to wear a pet boa constrictor around his neck while on stage. While he was rehearsing in his hotel room, the snake started to constrict Cooper's neck. A bodyguard couldn't get the snake to uncoil, so he took out a pocketknife and cut off its head.

> At a 1965 concert in Sacramento, Keith Richards smashed his microphone with the neck of his guitar. It produced a giant bolt of electricity that sent him flying through the air and then knocked him on his back, unconscious. Two minutes later, he came to. He credited his survival to the thick soles of the suede Hush Puppy boots he was wearing at the time.

In 1971, Kinks guitarist Dave Davies tried to steal a french fry from one of his brothers, singer Ray Davies. In retaliation, Ray stabbed Dave in the chest with a fork.

> Rehearsing a stage act in 1988, Alice Cooper nearly hung himself when a safety rope broke and the noose around his neck tightened. He would have died if a roadie hadn't cut him free.

> While Nirvana performed the song "Lithium" at the 1992 MTV awards show, bassist Novoselic tossed his bass in the air. It came down and hit him on the head, temporarily knocking him out. Kurt Cobain apparently missed the accident and screamed at him for being off beat.

Janis Joplin's final request was for her friends to have a farewell party at her favorite bar. She even left $2,500 to sponsor the party.

> Jimi Hendrix, the rock guitarist, died in London on September 18, 1970. The cause of death was drinking a barbiturate-and-alcohol cocktail.

> The worst catastrophe in rock history was hosted by the Who in 1979. Booked at the Riverfront Stadium in Cincinnati, Ohio, the band watched as a crowd rushed the stadium doors before the show. Eleven fans were crushed and killed in the melee. After the show, Roger Daltry is said to have cried his eyes out.

THIS IS THE END

The most visited cemetery in the world is the Cimetière du Père Lachaise in Paris. Established in 1805, the lush grounds contain the tombs of more than 1 million people. The most visited tomb, however, is that of the Doors' lead singer, Jim Morrison, who died of a drug overdose in France in 1971.

Reincarnations?

Born As...	Known As...
Robert Van Winkle	Vanilla Ice
Ellen Naomi Cohen	Mama Cass Elliot
Declan Patrick McManus	Elvis Costello
Vincent Furnier	Alice Cooper
Robert Zimmerman	Bob Dylan
Henry John Deutschendorf, Jr.	John Denver
Reginald Kenneth Dwight	Elton John
Arnold Dorsey	Engelbert Humperdinck
Annie Mae Bullock	Tina Turner
Brian Warner	Marilyn Manson

Gordon Sumner, the rock star and actor known as Sting, got his nickname from the yellow-and-black jerseys he used to wear, which fellow musicians thought made him look like a bumble bee. Singer Johnny Cash was born J. R. Cash. He chose the first name John when the military wouldn't accept just initials on its forms.

Course 650: **No Satisfaction**

> Counting Crow lead singer Adam Duritz recalled in a 2000 interview that Rolling Stone Keith Richards once reprimanded him for sipping chicken soup to cure a cold—and instead gave him a bottle of Guinness.
> Mick Jagger had an emerald chip put in the middle of his upper-right incisor, but people thought it was spinach. He changed it to a ruby until he got tired of people discussing the drop of blood on his tooth. Jagger finally settled on a diamond.
> Mick Jagger was under the impression he was the father of Bebe Buell's daughter Liv. Eventually Bebe informed him Liv's father was Aerosmith's Steven Tyler. Liv Tyler now enjoys a successful acting career.

Bad boy Mick Jagger actually had a very conventional childhood. An excellent student, Jagger majored in European history and literature at the prestigious London School of Economics before dropping out to form the Rolling Stones. He was the son of a gym teacher.

> The fuzz box was invented to give the guitar a unique "saxophonic" sound. The small box was operated by foot; when connected to the instrument, it put out a fuzzy distorted sound that "filled" gaps. The fuzz box gained instant fame in the rock world when the Rolling Stones used it in their 1965 hit "Satisfaction," and it was used by most musicians of the era thereafter.
> Rock superstar Mick Jagger sang backup for Carly Simon's hit "You're So Vain," the song supposedly written about Warren Beatty.

Music and Coke

Over the decades, the Coca-Cola company signed on some big names in the entertainment industry to push its bubbly beverage. Recording artists who have endorsed Coke include Roy Orbison, Jan and Dean, Diana Ross, Ray Charles, the Beach Boys, the Temptations, the Drifters, the Moody Blues, and the Guess Who.

Course 651: **Who Would Have Guessed?**

> While it's well-known that Stevie Wonder's first big hit, "Fingertips," was released when he was just 13, only his lawyers know for sure that the singer-musician endorses all contracts with his fingerprint. A case of blind faith?
> Pop duo Ike and Tina Turner have been inducted into the Rock and Roll Hall of Fame—but Sonny and Cher have not.

> Before he became famous for his TV comedy work, the late Phil Hartman was a talented and respected graphic designer. In fact, he was the designer of the logo for Crosby, Stills, Nash, and Young.

> As of 2000, comedienne and writer Phyllis Diller has appeared as a piano soloist with 100 symphony orchestras across the United States, including orchestras in Dallas, Denver, Annapolis, Houston, Baltimore, Pittsburgh, Detroit, and Cincinnati.

The Bee Gees became so desperate to sell records that they gave members of their fan club money to go out and buy albums. There were only 6 people in the fan club at that time.

> Gene Simmons, of the shock-rock group Kiss, earned a B.A. in education and speaks 4 languages.

> Parody singer and composer "Weird" Al Yankovich earned an architecture degree from California Polytechnic State University.

> Warner Communications paid $28 million for the copyright to the song "Happy Birthday."

> "Happy Birthday" was the first song to be performed in outer space. It was sung by the Apollo IX astronauts on March 8, 1969.

Reportedly, country singer Dolly Parton has her breasts insured for $600,000.

> The only member of the rock group ZZ Top that did not have a beard was named Frank. His last name, of course, was Beard.

> Irving Berlin never learned to read or write music. He hummed or sang his songs to a secretary, who wrote them down in musical notation.

> Stephen Stills, who went on to join Crosby, Stills, and Nash, originally tried out to be a Monkee. He didn't get the part. Producers felt that he was losing too much hair and that his teeth were too bad.

Crosby, Stills, Nash, and Young electrified the nation back in 1969 with "Ohio," their tune protesting the student shootings at Kent State. Slightly less electrifying is the fact that "Hang On Sloopy" is the official rock song of the state of Ohio.

Five Name Bands

1. The popular band the Police was originally known as Strontium 90.

2. The rock band REO Speedwagon chose its unusual name from an early 1900s flatbed truck. The letters REO are the initials of Ransom Eli Olds, "Father of the Automobile," who invented the Oldsmobile.

3. The rock group Jethro Tull is named after the eighteenth-century Englishman who invented the seed drill.

4. Jim Morrison found the name the Doors for his rock band in the title of Aldous Huxley's book *The Doors of Perception*, which extolls the use of hallucinogenic drugs.

5. When David Crosby, Graham Nash, and Stephen Stills first started singing together, they were called the Frozen Noses in honor of unique harmonies and rumored drug habits.

Course 663: **Classical Arrangements**

> As a child, Beethoven made such a poor impression on his music teachers that he was pronounced hopeless as a composer. Even Haydn, who taught him harmony, did not recognize Beethoven's potential genius.

> The British Broadcasting Company played the opening bars of Beethoven's *Fifth Symphony* in all its broadcasts to Europe during World War II. The familiar "dah-dah-dah-DAAAAH" opening is the same as Morse code for the letter *v* (dot-dot-dot-dash)—the symbol adopted for "victory."

> Through analyzing Beethoven's hair, historian Russell Martin concluded, "His deafness, illness, and death were almost certainly the result of lead poisoning." Martin further speculates that this may have resulted from lead pencils—on which Ludwig was munching while composing music.

> The majestic Hapsburgs' Schonbrunn Palace in Vienna has 1,441 rooms, of which 40 are opened to public tours. At age six, Wolfgang Amadeus Mozart performed for the royals in this palace.

Mozart once composed a piano piece that required a player to use two hands and his nose in order to hit all the correct notes.

> The national anthem of Austria was composed by Wolfgang Mozart.

> The composer of the ballet *The Nutcracker*, Peter Ilyich Tchaikovsky, wasn't that fond of the commission. What has become one of the most recognizable ballet scores in the world was, according to Tchaikovsky, "infinitely worse than *Sleeping Beauty*."

Peter Ilyich Tchaikovsky was supported by a wealthy widow for 13 years. She stipulated that they never meet, and they didn't.

Course 674: **The Fab Four**

> John Lennon was born on October 9, 1940, at Oxford Maternity Hospital in Liverpool, England, during an air raid.

> According to Beatles producer George Martin, Neal Hefti's catchy, Emmy Award–winning theme song for the 1960s *Batman* series inspired George Harrison to write the hit song "Taxman."
> On November 23, 1969, four years after receiving it, John Lennon sent back his Most Excellent Order of the British Empire (MBE) award. He stated that he was returning the MBE in protest against British involvement in Biafra, Nigeria, and Vietnam.

At the end of the Beatles' song "A Day in the Life," an ultrasonic whistle audible only to dogs was recorded specially by Paul McCartney for his Shetland sheepdog. No wonder your beagle loves the Beatles!

> In the early 1960s, opinionist William F. Buckley, Jr., wrote: "The Beatles are not merely awful, I would consider it sacrilegious to say anything less than that they are godawful. . . . They are so unbelievably horrible, so appallingly unmusical, so dogmatically insensitive to the magic of the art, that they qualify as crowned heads of anti-music."
> The Beatles' first #1 hit song was the 1964 "Love Me Do."
> The Beatles held the top 5 spots on the April 4, 1964 *Billboard* singles chart. To date, they're the only band to have ever accomplished that feat.

"We don't like their sound, and guitar music is on the way out"—Decca Recording Company on rejecting the Beatles, 1962

> "A Hard Day's Night," the now-famous title song of the Beatles' debut feature-length film, was written after the movie had completed filming.
> On September 23, 1969, the tabloid *The Northern Star* printed the first of many rumors that Beatle singer Paul McCartney was dead. Its first shocking headline read "Clues Hint at Beatle Death," which created an outbreak of speculative and near-hysterical opinions, most of which were pulled from interpretations of Beatle album covers and song lyrics. Teenage girls all over the world were in a frenzy for months.

The song "Back in the U.S.S.R." (1968) was originally written for model Twiggy to record, but the Beatles decided to keep it and use the song themselves.

> "Long Tall Sally" was the last song played by the Beatles during their last scheduled concert, which took place at Candlestick Park in San Francisco on August 29, 1966.
> The song "Hey Bulldog" on the Beatles' album *Yellow Submarine* was the last song John Lennon and Paul McCartney wrote in full collaboration. Oddly enough, while the song was on the album, it wasn't used in the film of the same title.
> In 1994, singer/musician Paul McCartney sent back his razor, shaving cream, and other products to the Gillette Co. to protest the manufacturer's use of

animals in its product testing. In his letter to Gillette's chief executive, the former Beatle demanded a refund, which he said he would donate to People for the Ethical Treatment of Animals.

> Paul McCartney urged those mourning his late wife, Linda, to "go veggie" since she was a well-known vegetarian.

Ex-Beatle Paul McCartney sang under the alias Apollo C. Vermouth.

> John Lennon joined Elton John onstage at Madison Square Garden in 1974 to perform the song they cowrote, "Whatever Gets You Through the Night." This was to be Lennon's final live performance.

> On November 12, 1995, NBC's *Mad About You* featured the acting debut of 62-year-old Yoko Ono, who once was universally blamed for the breakup of the Beatles. The show's star and cocreator Paul Reiser had been coaxing John Lennon's widow to appear for more than two years.

Paul McCartney said in a 1995 interview that he was sick of living in John Lennon's shadow: "There are certain people who think he was the Beatles. Now, that is not true, and John would be the first to tell you that."

> Paul McCartney had 32 #1 hits on the *Billboard* charts. That's more than any other artist.

> Following his breakup with the Beatles in 1971, Paul McCartney formed his group Wings. The group was nameless until McCartney, awaiting the birth of his daughter Stella about a month later, prayed for her health. He came up with the group's name on the "wings of an angel."

> George Harrison, with "My Sweet Lord," was the first Beatle to have a #1 hit single following the group's breakup.

In 1996, former Beatle drummer Ringo Starr appeared in a Japanese advertisement for applesauce, which coincidentally is what his name means in Japanese.

> More than 2,500 cover versions of the Beatles' "Yesterday" are in existence, making it the most recorded song in history.

> Trident Studios in London was the site of the recording of the Beatles' longest #1 hit single, "Hey Jude," written by Paul McCartney for John Lennon's son. Nearly all their other single recordings had taken place at EMI Studios, Abbey Road, London.

> Ringo Starr started out as Richard Starkey. While Starkey was in the band Skiffle, their front man Rory Storm dubbed him Rings because he wore so many rings. Storm eventually changed the nickname to Ringo to give it a cowboy flavor.

Zak Starkey, son of drummer Ringo Starr, is now the drummer for the legendary band the Who.

Senior Music Quiz

1. The David Bowie band, Tin Machine, features two children of comedian...

    a) Jerry Lewis
    b) Rodney Dangerfield
    c) Soupy Sales
    d) Johnny Carson

2. The eerie sounds of what musical instrument can be heard in Alfred Hitchcock's SPELLBOUND and the Beach Boys' "Good Vibrations"?

    a) theremin
    b) mellotron
    c) Moog synthesizer
    d) clavivox

3. The line "Play it Again, Sam" refers to what song in the classic movie CASABLANCA?

    a) "As Time Goes By"
    b) "Time After Time"
    c) "Time of the Season"
    d) "Time Is on Your Side"

4. In 1955, the original anthem of the rock 'n' roll era, "Rock Around the Clock," was recorded by...

    a) Steve Smith and the Satellites
    b) Bill Haley and the Comets
    c) Mike Rodgers and the Rockets
    d) Jerry Lee Lewis

5. From what book did Steely Dan get their name?

    a) *Lord of the Flies*
    b) *Catcher in the Rye*
    c) *Huckleberry Finn*
    d) *Naked Lunch*

ANSWERS

1.c 2.a 3.a 4.b 5.d

Amaze Your Friends!

Everyone knows the film *Fantasia,* but be the first person on your block to know that a *fantasia* is a piece of music of an improvisational character, with the composition following the fancy rather than any conventional form.

And in case anyone asks, a *zarzuela* is an operetta of a traditional type, with spoken dialogue and lyrical music. The word is derived from the Spanish after La Zarzuela, the royal palace near Madrid where the operetta was first performed in 1629. *Zarzuela* is also the name of a seafood stew.

Oh yes, by the way, in music, a *hemidemisemiquaver* is a sixty-fourth note. *Zapateodo* is a rhythmic device used in flamenco music; and the musical term *scherzo* comes from an Italian word for "prank."

Course 688: **The First**

> The first jukebox was installed at the Palais Royal Hotel in San Francisco in 1899.
> In December 1925, American composer George Gershwin appeared as a soloist at a concert in New York's Carnegie Hall. He played his *Concerto in F,* the first jazz concerto for piano in musical history.
> Richard Rodgers and Oscar Hammerstein II wrote the first musical about Chinese-Americans, *Flower Drum Song* (1958).
> In 1965, at age 30, Loretta Lynn became country music's first female millionaire.

The cover of the very first issue of *Rolling Stone* magazine featured John Lennon.

> During their 1976 tour, the Who became the first rock group to use lasers in a live performance.
> In 1977, the Nitty Gritty Dirt Band became the first American pop group to tour the U.S.S.R.
> In 1990, Irish rock singer Sinéad O'Connor became the first musical recording artist to refuse a Grammy Award, which she won for her recording of, ironically enough, "I Do Not Want What I Haven't Got." She claimed that too much emphasis was placed on the pop charts, and not enough on the ills and abuses of the world.
> At a ceremony in the Waldorf-Astoria in 1998, Carlos Santana became the first Hispanic to be inducted into the Rock and Roll Hall of Fame.

As a result of Russian copyright law changes in 1975, the Rolling Stones became the first rock group to receive Russian royalties.

New Names, Sudden Fame

They were originally...	But became...
Carl and the Passions	The Beach Boys
Johnny and the Moondogs	The Beatles
New Yardbirds	Led Zeppelin
Salty Peppers	Earth, Wind, and Fire
Tom and Jerry	Simon and Garfunkel
Rattlesnakes	The Bee Gees

Course 690: **Slightly Spaced Out?**

> Beach Boy Brian Wilson spent the years from 1971 to 1975 in bed.
> Singer Glen Campbell substituted for Brian Wilson during the Beach Boys' 1965 tour.

John Denver was a pilot who had a desire to see outer space. He campaigned to fly the 1986 *Challenger* mission, but was turned down. The Russians offered to let him fly their next space mission—for $10 million. Across America, disc jockeys took up collections to buy Denver a one-way ticket into space.

> U2's Bono has a habit of losing things, from keys to checks, but he had real problems when he lost the lyrics to all the songs for their album *October*. U2 still recorded the album; Bono says he didn't know what he was saying most of the time.

It is rock music legend that recording *Rumours,* Fleetwood Mac was so strung out on cocaine that they spent four days trying to tune a piano. They went so far as to bring in nine different pianos before deciding not to include any piano music whatsoever. Fleetwood Mac also performed Bill Clinton's campaign song at his inaugural ball. Are these facts related?

Sir Elton

Elton John has been reported to go on legendary shopping sprees. There have been rumors that he spent $85,000 and up on Versace outfits, and it is said he once spent $850,000 in one day's worth of shopping.

Elton's handwritten lyrics for his televised funeral tribute to Princess Diana were sold at auction for $442,500 in February 1998. The money from the revised "Candle in the Wind 1997," also known as "Goodbye England's Rose," went to several of the princess's charities. The lyrics were modified from his Marilyn Monroe–inspired pop hit song.

The question is: why didn't he give up one day of shopping and donate that money to Princess Diana's charities instead? Hmmm…

Course 691: **A Whiter Shade of Pale**

> Michael Jackson went to Disneyland three to four times dressed in costumes to blend in with the crowd. He would wear hats, wigs, and fake beards and noses, but eventually he gave up the disguises. Instead, he went in a wheelchair so that he could get to the front of the lines first.
> Michael Jackson used to keep 6 mannequins in his bedroom. They were dressed in evening gowns and boas, and he gave them names. Jackson's comment: "I like to imagine talking to them."

There was a simple reason Michael Jackson wrapped three of his fingers in surgical tape; he heard Howard Hughes used to do it.

> To those of you residing in the city of Charleston or along the Chattanooga River: please remember that Michael Jackson owns the rights to the South Carolina state anthem.
> In March 1986, Michael Jackson received the biggest sponsorship deal to date from Pepsi-Cola. He was paid $15 million up front to appear in two TV commercials, and Pepsi agreed to sponsor his first solo tour. Also, a 1984 Pepsi sponsorship of $7 million was split among the other Jackson brothers.
> Michael Jackson was the seventh child in a family of 9 children.
> Two life-threatening brain aneurysms in 1974 terminated Quincy Jones's horn-playing days, but not his musical talents. Jones went on to produce Michael Jackson's *Off the Wall*, *Thriller*, and *Bad*, as well as the ambitious all-star hit "We Are the World" in 1985. Jones has composed more than 24 film scores and won more than 26 Grammys.

Liberated Liberace

Flamboyant entertainer Liberace owned 39 pianos; 18 of his rarest instruments are on display in the Piano Gallery at the Liberace Museum in Las Vegas, Nevada. One of the most notable pianos in the collection is Chopin's French Pleyel. Liberace's favorite Baldwin concert grand piano, covered with thousands of etched mirror tiles, is also on display.

What's more, Liberace's elaborately ornate cars are showcased in the Car Gallery, including a one-of-a-kind Rolls Royce covered with mirror tiles etched with galloping horses. The exotic Rolls is a Phantom V Landau limousine with a James Young body and Deville extension. Only 7 were made, and it is the only one with left-hand steering.

Course 697: **Higher Notes?**

> "I'd rather be dead than singing when I'm 45."—Mick Jagger
> Dimitri Tiomkin wrote *High Noon*'s prize-winning musical score. Asked how a Russian-born concert pianist could write Western music, Tiomkin had a quick reply. "Did Strauss," he inquired hotly, "have to be an Olympic swimmer to write 'The Blue Danube'?"
> During the 1989 invasion of Panama, U.S. troops blared out AC/DC's "Highway to Hell" at the highest volume possible to drive Manuel Noriega out of the Vatican Embassy. When vocalist Brian Johnson heard that his music was being used as psychological torture, he is quoted as saying, "I guess now we won't get to play for the Pope."

In a 1992 MTV interview, Eddie Van Halen said playing the guitar wasn't as hard as brain surgery. A few days later, he got a letter from a brain surgeon offering surgery lessons in exchange for guitar lessons.

> About current music, veteran show-tune composer Alan Jay Lerner was heard to say: "Youth has many glories, but judgment is not one of them, and no amount of electronic amplification can turn a belch into an aria."
> Emperor Ferdinand of Austria once commented: "Far too noisy, my dear Mozart. Far too many notes."
> "It is a sobering thought that when Mozart was my age, he had been dead for two years."—Tom Lehrer

Cher said about herself: "I'm the female equivalent of a counterfeit 20-dollar bill. Half of what you see is a pretty good reproduction, and the rest is a fraud."

> "If I had done everything I'm credited with, I'd be speaking to you from a laboratory jar at Harvard," remarked Frank Sinatra.

"Rock journalism is people who can't write interviewing people who can't talk for people who can't read."—Frank Zappa

> According to John Lennon, "Life is what happens when you are making other plans."
> Originally a DJ, Luther Campbell of 2 Live Crew nicknamed himself Luke Skywalker after the *Star Wars* character. When the group got publicity for their explicit lyrics, *Star Wars* creator George Lucas took legal action to keep Campbell from using the character's name. Luther pouted, "George Lucas showed me his dark side."

When the TV musical group the Monkees had their first dinner together, Davy Jones was appalled by Mickey Dolenz's table manners. Jones said Dolenz "ate like a pig." Dolenz's response was to grab two handfuls of salad and stuff them into his mouth.

> While punk rocker Courtney Love was in labor with her and Kurt Cobain's child, he was in the rehab wing of the same hospital. Courtney shocked her doctors by walking out of the delivery room to get Cobain out of his room. She yelled at him, "You are not leaving me to do this by myself!" Cobain joined her in the delivery room, but when the baby's head appeared, he vomited and passed out.
> Neil Diamond once walked around Australia wearing a shirt that said, "I'm not Neil Diamond—I just look like him." David Samson (coauthor of this book) once walked around Beverly Hills wearing a shirt that said, "I am Neil Diamond—I just don't look like him."

Final Exam

1. The popular jingle "I'm a Pepper, you're a Pepper, wouldn't you like to be a Pepper too?" was written by Brian Wilson of the Beachboys.

True or False?

2. Stevie Wonder was 11 years old when he signed his first record contract with Motown.

True or False?

3. Burt Bacharach started his musical career as an organ grinder on the boardwalk in Coney Island.

True or False?

4. Eric Clapton attended Kingston College of Art, and his original career path was stained-glass design.

True or False?

5. The largest, most complicated musical instrument is the piano.

True or False?

6. The original title of Leonard Bernstein's brilliant musical *West Side Story* was *East Side Story*.

True or False?

7. The Ramones claimed they played so incredibly loudly at a 1977 concert in Marseilles, France, that the power drain caused a blackout across the city.

True or False?

8. Pop music stars who were buried in ornate aboveground crypts include Kurt Cobain, Jerry Garcia, John Denver, Woody Guthrie, Janis Joplin, John Lennon, Curtis Mayfield, Marvin Gaye, Maria Callas, Dusty Springfield, and Sid Vicious.

True or False?

9. The Beatles were the first British group to hit the #1 spot on the American record charts.

True or False?

10. At one time, Jon Bon Jovi cleaned dog kennels, and Cindy Lauper was a floor sweeper.

True or False?

ANSWERS

1. FALSE. It was written by Barry Alan Pincus, better known as Barry Manilow. Early in his career, Manilow wrote commercial jingles for State Farm, Dr. Pepper, Kentucky Fried Chicken, Pepsi, McDonald's, and Band-Aid brand band-aids. He even recorded a medley of his commercial jingles titled "A Very Strange Medley (V.S.M.)."

2. TRUE.

3. FALSE. He was an accompanist for singer Vic Damone—and was fired.

4. TRUE. The blues-obsessed youth was expelled at age 17 for playing his guitar in an art class. Clapton worked as a manual laborer, and spent most of his spare time strumming the electric guitar he had persuaded his grandparents to purchase for him.

5. FALSE. It's the organ, which has been the primary instrument used for church music since the fourth century.

6. TRUE.

7. TRUE.

8. FALSE. They were all cremated.

9. FALSE. On December 22, 1962, "Telstar," by the Tornadoes, became the first UK single to reach number one in the United States. It was not until February 1, 1964, that the Fab Four made it to #1 in the States with "I Want to Hold Your Hand."

10. FALSE. Just the reverse is true.

8

The USELESS
School of
Geography

Featuring the Environmental Institute

Amaze your friends and confound your enemies by asking them what every continent on the planet has in common. It's child's play! The first letter of every continent's name is the same as the last: AmericA, AntarcticA, EuropE, AsiA, AustraliA, AfricA. Let's face it—everyone hates geography. Detroit is located in Michigan, for instance. Frankly, wouldn't you rather replace that item with the fact that Petosky, Michigan, is famous for Petosky Stones. What are Petosky Stones? Prehistoric and fossilized coral that predates even the Reagan administration!

Naturally, as a sophisticated world traveler, you can pooh-pooh the tired old cities of London, Rome, or even Paris, and impress everyone with the fact that you've grown rather fond of exotic locales such as Nez Perce, Coeur d'Alene, and Cataldo. Everyone will be too embarrassed to ask you where they are, which is just as well since they're all located in Ohio.

That's right. Useless Geography Replacement Therapy has infinite possibilities. Rave about Antelope Island State Park. Where? It's right in the middle of the Great Salt Lake in Utah. Rhapsodize over the Shirley Mountains and Rattlesnake Hills of Wyoming. Or maybe you're just going nowhere—that's okay, too. It just so happens that Nowhere is the actual name of a town in Oklahoma.

Remember: even if you're a couch potato, this is the one course in geography that is designed to get under your skin!

Course 701:

Highest, Largest, Longest, and Greatest

> The Bingham Canyon copper mine in Utah is the biggest manmade hole on Earth. It is more than half a mile deep and 2.5 miles across. An astronaut can see this hole from the space shuttle with his bare eyes.
> The world's biggest meteor crater is located in New Quebec, Canada.
> Of the 25 highest mountains on Earth, 19 are in the Himalayas.
> The highest point in the contiguous 48 states is in California: Mount Whitney, which is 14,491 feet above sea level.

The highest point in Pennsylvania is lower than the lowest point in Colorado.

> The border between Canada and the United States is the world's longest frontier. It stretches 3,987 miles (6,416 kilometers).
> The Salto Alto (Angel Falls) in Venezuela is the highest waterfall known. It is more than twenty times higher than Niagara Falls.

Australia's Ayers Rock is the largest rock in the world. It has a diameter of 5 miles around its base and a height of 1,000 feet.

> Lake Superior is the world's largest lake. The Great Lakes themselves have a combined area of 94,230 square miles—larger than that of the states of New York, New Jersey, Connecticut, Rhode Island, Massachusetts, and Vermont combined.

> Strangeray Springs cattle station in South Australia is the largest ranch in the world. Its area measures 30,029 square kilometers—only slightly smaller than the area of Belgium.

The Nile is the world's longest river—even longer than the Amazon. If the Nile River were stretched across the United States, it would run almost from New York to Los Angeles.

> The King Ranch in Texas is bigger than the state of Rhode Island. It comprises 1.25 million acres and was the first ranch in the world to be completely fenced in.

> The state that has the longest coastline in the United States is Alaska. It measures 6,640 miles, greater than those of all the other 49 states combined.

The smallest county in America is New York County—better known as Manhattan. Despite its small size, Manhattan undoubtedly contains many of the country's biggest egos.

Know Where Your Country Is?

According to the National Geographic Society, a survey of 18- to 24-year-olds from nine nations put the United States dead last in general geographic knowledge scores. One in 7—about 24 million people—could not even find their own country on a world map. The survey revealed that Americans possess a pathetically poor sense of where they are—much less any knowledge about the rest of the world. And even more alarming, those who participated in the survey were recent high school and college graduates.

Course 708:
Lowest, Deepest, Shortest, and Smallest

> The world's shortest river—the D River in Oregon—is only 121 feet long.
> The Netherlands are the lowest country in the world. It is estimated that 40 percent of the land is below sea level.
> At 282 feet below sea level, Badwater, in Death Valley, is the lowest point in the Western Hemisphere.

The Dead Sea is the lowest body of water on Earth. It is 1,315 feet below sea level at its lowest point.

> The deepest trench in the world is the Mariana Trench in the Pacific Ocean at a depth of 36,201 feet. The second-deepest trench is the Tonga Trench, also in the Pacific Ocean. It is 35,430 feet deep.
> Located 137 miles northeast of Rome, San Marino is the oldest republic in the world, and one of the smallest.
> The wettest location in the United States is Mount Waialeale on the Hawaiian island of Kauai. It receives around 480 inches of rain each year. Death Valley, California, gets only 1.5 inches per year.
> Nauru, an island in Oceania, is the smallest independent republic in the world. It is about one-tenth the size of Washington, D.C., and had an estimated population of 11,845 in July 2000.
> Monaco is so small it covers about 350 acres. Fifty-five Monacos could fit inside the city of Paris; the whole country could squeeze into half of Central Park in New York City.
> Lake Tahoe in California is the deepest (at 1,645 feet) and the largest mountain lake in North America.

Israel is one-quarter the size of the state of Maine.

> Hell's Canyon on the Snake River is deeper than the Grand Canyon.

RHODE ISLAND TAKE HEART!

As small as the state of Rhode Island is with its 1,214 square miles, there are six sovereign European states that are smaller. In alphabetical order, they are Andorra (290.8 square miles), Liechtenstein (99.4 square miles), Malta (196.3 square miles), Monaco (1.2 square miles), San Marino (37.6 square miles), and Vatican City (0.17 square miles).

Course 717:
Driest, Wettest, Hottest, and Coldest

> The world's coldest inhabited place is Norilsk, Russia, where the average temperature is 12.4° Fahrenheit (–10.9° Celsius). Located in the Rybnaya Valley, Norilsk experiences 5 months without sunlight because of its polar location.

> The hottest inhabited place on the planet is Djibouti, capital of the Republic of Djibouti, Africa, where the average temperature is 86° Fahrenheit (30° Celsius). The second-hottest place is Timbuktu, Mali, where the average temperature is 84.7° Fahrenheit (29.3° Celsius).

> The world's driest inhabited region is Aswan, Egypt. The southernmost city in Egypt, it averages only .02 inches (.5 millimeter) of rain per year.

The worst climate in the world may be at Yakutsk, in Russia. In winter, the temperature falls to -84° Fahrenheit. In summer, it can reach 102° Fahrenheit.

> The world's wettest inhabited place is Buenaventura, Colombia. It gets about 265 inches (673 centimeters) of rain a year thanks to its location near the South American jungles on the Pacific coast.

> In Siberia, it can get so cold that the moisture in a person's breath freezes instead of forming vapor. It can actually be heard when it falls to the ground as ice crystals.

Hell, Michigan, was in the news during the extremely cold winter of 1995–96—when it froze over.

Quiz: What State Are You In?

1. Which state is considered the vampire capital of the United States—
Rhode Island or Virginia?

2. Which state does Yellowstone National Park cross into from Wyoming—
Montana or Idaho?

3. Which state has a house built by a former U.S. consul to Hawaii, known as the Honolulu House—
Hawaii or Michigan?

4. Which state contains Bemidji, the legendary home of Paul Bunyan—
Pennsylvania or Minnesota?

5. If you're traveling down the Cripple Creek, which state are you in—
Colorado or North Carolina?

6. Which state has the Ginkgo Petrified Forest State Park—
New Mexico or Washington?

7. Which state is known as the Beaver State—
Oregon or West Virginia?

8. Which state contains Sunset Crater Volcano National Monument—
North Dakota or Arizona?

9. If you're walking on the Confusion Range, which state are you in—
Utah or South Carolina?

10. If you're wandering the Desolation Wilderness, which state are you in—
Nevada or California?

ANSWERS

1. Rhode Island **2.** Montana **3.** Michigan **4.** Minnesota **5.** Colorado **6.** Washington **7.** Oregon **8.** Arizona **9.** Utah **10.** California

Course 726: **The Most**

> Bangladesh is the most densely populated non-island region in the world, with more than 1,970 humans per square mile.
> The most densely populated state in the United States is New Jersey.
> Filled with water, gas, electric, telephone, cable, steam, and sewer lines, Manhattan has the most dense underground in the United States.

Florida averages the largest number of shark attacks annually— an average of 13.

> Hawaii (not Florida) is the southernmost state in the United States. It is also the only U.S. state that lies below the Tropic of Cancer.
> Yuma, Arizona, has the most sun of any locale in the United States—it averages sunny skies 332 days a year.
> Per square mile, Oklahoma has the most tornadoes of all U.S. states.

Seen the Seven Wonders?

The 7 wonders of the natural world are:

1. Mount Everest in Nepal/Tibet

2. Victoria Falls in Zambia/Zimbabwe

3. The Grand Canyon in Arizona

4. The Great Barrier Reef in Australia

5. The northern lights

6. Paricutin Volcano in Mexico

7. Rio de Janeiro Harbor in Brazil

Course 735: **The Only**

> Panama, because of a bend in the isthmus, is the only place in the world where one can see the sun rise on the Pacific Ocean and set on the Atlantic.
> Antarctica is the only continent without reptiles or snakes.
> Lebanon is the only country in the Middle East that does not have a desert.

Montpelier, Vermont, is the only U.S. state capital without a McDonald's.

> The only active diamond mine in the United States is in Arkansas.
> The only foreign country that has a capital city named after an American president is Liberia in Africa. The capital is Monrovia, named after James Monroe.
> Lake Baikal in Siberia is the only lake in the world that is deep enough to have deep-sea fish.
> The national anthems of Japan, Jordan, and San Marino each have only four lines.

The Bledowska Desert in Poland is the only desert in Europe.

> Maine is the only U.S. state that adjoins only one other state.
> From the 1830s to the 1960s, the Lehigh River in eastern Pennsylvania was owned by the Lehigh Coal and Navigation Co., making it the only privately owned river in the United States.

LIFE IS A BEACH

There's only one city in the United States named merely Beach. It is in North Dakota, which is a landlocked state.

Course 742: A Rose by Any Other Name...

> Taiwan was known formerly as Formosa.
> Ceylon became a republic in 1972 and changed its name to Sri Lanka. Located in the Indian Ocean just north of the equator, Sri Lanka had a highly developed civilization as early as the fifth century B.C.

The planner of the city of Washington, D.C., was French architect Pierre L'Enfant. At the time of its founding in 1791, it was known as Federal City.

> Originally, Pakistan was comprised of two separate land areas located about 1,000 miles apart to the east and west of India. The eastern portion seceded in 1971 as the independent nation of Bangladesh.
> Rhodesia in Africa was named after Cecil Rhodes, an Englishman who encouraged European whites to settle in Africa. Present-day southern Rhodesia is called Zimbabwe, and northern Rhodesia in Zambia.
> The modern city of Istanbul was formerly known as Byzantium, and then as Constantinople.

Lutetia was the ancient name of Paris, France.

> The old Roman province of Lusitania is now called Portugal. Some parts of
  Lusitania are also found in Spain.
> The ancient African kingdom of Abyssinia was later renamed Ethiopia.

WHAT IT REALLY MEANS

Thailand means "land of the free."
Kuwait's name is derived from *kut*, the Arabic word for "fort."
The city of San Juan used to be known as Puerto Rico (which means "rich
port" in Spanish).
Translated, *Siberia* means "sleeping land."
Honolulu means "sheltered harbor."
The translation of *Sri Lanka* is "beautiful country."

> In 1847, the coastal city of Yorba Buena in California changed its name to
  San Francisco. The city took its new name from St. Francis of Assisi, who is
  reconized as San Francisco's patron saint.
> Belize was formerly known as British Honduras.

**Saigon, the capital of South Vietnam, officially became Ho
Chi Minh City when the Communists took over the country.
Ho Chi Minh was a prominent Communist leader at the time.**

> Afghanistan has been known by different names. It was called Ariana or
  Bactria in ancient times and Khorasan during the Middle Ages.
> In 1997, Zaire, one of the largest countries in Africa, changed its name to
  the Democratic Republic of Congo.

**In 1507, the first globular map was published that showed the
Western Hemisphere. It was printed at St. Die in the Vosges
Mountains of Alsace and it was the first map to use the term *America*.**

Course 750: **Tales of the Islands**

> Hawaii's "Forbidden Island" of Niihau is owned by a single family named
  Robinson. On Niihau, there are no phones and no electricity for the 250
  full-blooded Hawaiians living there.
> Barking Sands Beach on the Hawaiian island of Kauai is known for its
  unusual sand, which squeaks or barks like a dog. The dry sand grains emit
  an eerie sound when rubbed with bare feet.

**The islands of Bermuda have no rivers or lakes. The inhabitants
must use rain for water.**

- Of the 3,000 islands of the Bahama chain in the Caribbean, only 20 are inhabited.
- At 840,000 square miles, Greenland is the largest island in the world. It is 3 times the size of Texas. By comparison, Iceland is only 39,800 square miles.
- The smallest island with country status is Pitcairn in Polynesia, at just 1.75 square miles (4.53 square kilometers).
- Japan consists of the four large islands of Hokkaido, Honshu, Shikoku, Kyushu, and about 3,000 smaller islands.

The Isle of Man (between Britain and Ireland) is rich in history, with Norse stone circles and long houses, signs of early Christianity, and evidence of man's first struggles to farm the land. This green, fertile land has its own currency, stamps, telecommunications, language, castles, legends, customs, and the oldest continuous parliament in the world.

- The Philippines is an archipelago of 7,107 islands in the Pacific Ocean. Finland has the greatest number of islands in the world: 179,584.
- About 43 million years ago, the Pacific plate took a northwest turn, creating a bend where new upheavals initiated the Hawaiian Ridge. Major islands formed included Kauai, 5.1 million years old, Maui, 1.3 million years old, and Hawaii, a youngster at only 800,000 years.
- The Spice Islands are now called the Moluccas, and they are located in eastern Indonesia between Celebes and New Guinea.

Oceania, sometimes called the South Seas, is the name for thousands of islands in the central and southern Pacific Ocean.

- A bar of sand or other sediment linking an island to the mainland or another island is called a *tombolo*.
- The island nation of Haiti is the world's oldest black republic. The major religion there is Voodoo.
- The time has come today? The islands of Hawaii have never adopted Daylight Savings Time. Neither have Puerto Rico, the Virgin Islands, or American Samoa.

26 MILES ACROSS THE SEA

Most of 76-square-mile Catalina Island, located off the California coast, is a park, forever barred from development. In 1975, the Wrigley family transferred 85 percent of the island to the Santa Catalina Island Conservancy, a nonprofit foundation dedicated to preserving and protecting open spaces, wild lands, and nature preserves. That means that what's wild in Catalina today will remain wild, including a large herd of buffalo. Avalon, the main settlement, has little room for expansion, so what's currently built is what will remain.

The 30 Weirdest Towns in America

1. Muck City, Alabama
2. Why, Arizona
3. Toad Suck, Arkansas
4. Yreka Zzyzx, California
5. Hygiene, Colorado
6. Okahumpka, Florida
7. Hopeulikit, Georgia
8. Beer Bottle Crossing, Idaho
9. Floyds Knobs, Indiana
10. Zurich, Kansas
11. Typo, Kentucky
12. Beans Corner Bingo, Maine
13. Gay, Michigan
14. Sanatorium, Mississippi
15. Frankenstein, Missouri
16. Square Butt, Montana
17. Elephant Butte, New Mexico
18. Tick Bite, North Carolina
19. Bowlegs, Oklahoma
20. Half.com, Oregon
21. Loyalsockville, Pennsylvania
22. Oral, South Dakota
23. Bucksnort, Tennessee
24. Ben Hur, Texas
25. Mosquitoville, Vermont
26. Satans Kingdom, Vermont
27. Clam, Virginia
28. Looneyville, West Virginia
29. Spread Eagle, Wisconsin
30. Camel Hump, Wyoming

The USELESS Environmental Institute

Next time someone complains that everyone talks about the weather, but no one can do anything about it, bring up the name of explorer Marco Polo. In his Asian travels, he discovered that Kublai Khan maintained 5,000 resident court astrologers. Their various duties included the hazardous task of weather prediction, with unforeseeable consequences for those who guessed wrong. Unfortunately, we have no such power over our present crop of TV weather people! That's right: weather is all around you—so now is the time to blow some major wind!

Course 768: Lightning Strikes

> A *fulgerite* is fossilized lightning. It forms when a powerful lightning bolt melts the soil into a glasslike state.

> A bolt of lightning travels at speeds of up to 100 million feet per second, or 72 million miles per hour.
> A lightning bolt generates temperatures five times hotter than the 6,000° centigrade found at the surface of the Sun.

According to Professor Walter Connor of the University of Michigan, men are six times more likely than women to be struck by lightning.

> Lightning kills more people in the United States than any other natural disaster: an average of 400 dead and 1,000 injured yearly. Florida is the state struck most often by lightning.

In Britain, two women were killed in 1999 by lightning conducted through their underwire bras, according to the West London Coroner's Office.

> Oak trees are struck by lightning more often than any other tree. It has been theorized that this is one reason that the ancient Greeks considered oak trees sacred to Zeus, god of thunder and lightning.
> On a clear day with blue skies, lightning can jump outside of its parent cloud and travel for more than five miles through clear air. This is called the bolt-from-the-blue phenomenon.

The study of lightning is called *keraunopathology*. Fear of lightning and thunder is called *astraphobia*.

Very Flakey

It only snows about 2 inches per year over most of Antarctica. It snows more at the Grand Canyon than it does in Minneapolis, Minnesota. Salt Lake City, Utah, gets an average of 17 inches more snow annually than Fairbanks, Alaska. Santa Fe, New Mexico, gets about 9 inches more snow each year than New Haven, Connecticut. Oh yes, dirty snow melts faster than clean.

Course 721: **Stormy Weather**

> The first hurricane given a male name was "Bob," in July 1979.
> The word *hurricane* is derived from the name of the West Indian god of storms, Huracan.
> A *pogonip* is a heavy winter fog containing ice crystals.

According to NASA, the United States has the world's most violent weather. In a typical year, the United States can expect some 10,000 violent thunderstorms, 5,000 floods, 1,000 tornadoes, and several hurricanes.

> A hurricane releases as much energy as the explosion of a Hiroshima-type atomic bomb.
> Hurricanes, cyclones, and typhoons spin counterclockwise north of the equator, and clockwise south of the equator. This is known as the *Coriolis Effect*.
> The low rumbling of distant thunder is called *brontide*.

On June 10, 1958, a tornado was crashing through El Dorado, Kansas. The storm pulled a woman out of her house and carried her 60 feet away. Reportedly, she landed, relatively unharmed, next to a phonograph record titled "Stormy Weather."

What a Waste!

Cars produce about 4 times their own weight in carbon dioxide each year. The average home produces 50 tons of carbon dioxide each year.

Disposable diapers in the United States make up enough trash to fill a barge half a city block long, every 6 hours, every day.

A plastic container can resist decomposition for as long as a million years.

Fingernail polish often contains 4 or 5 chemicals the EPA calls potentially harmful.

A leaking toilet can waste as much as 200 gallons of water a day without making a sound.

The junk mail that Americans receive in one day could produce enough energy to heat 250,000 homes.

A man shaving with a hand razor at the sink uses more household energy (because of the water power, the water pump, and so on) than he would by using an electric razor.

Three hundred and fourteen acres of trees are used to make the newsprint for the average Sunday edition of the *New York Times*. There are nearly 63,000 trees in the 314 acres. Let's see *that* on the editorial page!

TWO PIECES OF GOOD NEWS!

1. McDonald's Corporation eliminated 1 million pounds of waste per year in the 1980s by making their drinking straws 20 percent lighter.

2. More than 500 crematories in the United States are now considered environmentally friendly. They are engineered to have the vapors recirculated through the oven, so that little, if any, of a corpse's gases escape into the atmosphere.

Course 761: **Beautiful Visions**

> A captivating mirage called the fata morgana appears in the Straits of Messina, between Sicily and Italy. It is an image of a town in the sky, but it seems more like a fairy landscape than a real town. It is believed to be a mirage of a fishing village situated along the coast.

> A green flash is sometimes seen just as the sun sets or rises. This occurs because the atmosphere bends green light more strongly than light of other colors. So green is seen before other colors at sunrise, and after the other colors have vanished at sunset.

> A rainbow can be seen only in the morning or late afternoon. It is a phenomenon that can occur only when the Sun is 40° or lower above the horizon. When viewed from above, rainbows are doughnut shaped. According to Greek mythology, the goddess of rainbows was Iris.

The aurora borealis, the aurora of the Earth's Northern Hemisphere, is also called the northern lights. Less well-known is the fact that there is an aurora of the Southern Hemisphere called the *aurora australis,* also known as the southern lights.

Course 762: **Water Power**

> The gulf countries of the Middle East are located on the Arabian Gulf. It is important when visiting or conducting business in those countries to remember that—and not refer to the gulf as the Persian Gulf.

> If the Earth's surface were completely smoothed out, both above and below the water, the ocean would cover the entire globe to a depth of 12,000 feet.

> The deadliest flood of the twentieth century occurred in 1931 when the Yellow River in China flooded and 3.7 million people died.

Grasshopper Glacier in Montana was named for the grasshoppers that can still be seen frozen in the ice.

> Glaciers store about 75 percent of the world's freshwater. In Washington State alone, glaciers provide 470 billion gallons of water each summer.

> The Amazon River pushes so much water into the Atlantic that, more than a hundred miles at sea, off the mouth of the river, one can dip freshwater out of the ocean and drink it. The river's daily flow is three times the flow of all rivers in the United States combined.

Since 1901, 15 people have intentionally gone over the Canadian side of Niagara Falls. (Two people went over twice. Five have lost their lives.) The first person to go over the falls was Annie Edson-Taylor. She made the trip in a wooden barrel and survived.

> Majestic Niagara Falls, a popular honeymoon site for newlyweds that is located in both New York and Ontario, was named after the Mohawk Indian word meaning "thunder of waters." Though of great water volume, Niagara Falls has parallel drops of only 158 and 167 feet.

> There is only one river in the world that has its source near the equator and that flows from there into a temperate zone: the Nile. For some unknown reason, most rivers flow in the opposite direction.

Water is so scarce in the arid regions of China that in the grasslands the people never take baths and sometimes wash their faces in yak's milk.

> Lake Erie is about 326 feet higher than Lake Ontario, and the Welland Canal provides a navigable waterway between the two. The canal stretches 27 miles and uses 8 locks to raise and lower the ships. More than 3,000 ships pass through the waterway annually.

> The white cliffs of Dover are a natural landmark on the southern coast of England. Their distinctive color was created by the accumulation of skeletal remains of tiny organisms deposited over thousands of centuries. Sea level was higher millions of years ago, and after the waters receded, the whitish remains of the creatures were exposed.

The Caspian Sea and the Dead Sea are actually lakes.

> Ruby Falls, America's highest underground waterfall open to the public, is located on historic Lookout Mountain in Chattanooga, Tennessee.

> There are over 3 million lakes in Alaska. The largest, Lake Iliamna, is the size of Connecticut.

> Canada has more lakes than the rest of the world combined.

Course 765: **Blasts from the Past!**

> Although Mount Everest, at 29,028 feet, is often called the tallest mountain on Earth, Mauna Kea, an inactive volcano on the island of Hawaii, is actually taller. Only 13,796 feet of Mauna Kea stand above sea level, yet it is 33,465 feet tall if measured from the ocean floor to its summit.

> Four states have active volcanoes: Washington, California, Alaska, and Hawaii, whose Mauna Loa is the world's largest active volcano. Hawaii itself was formed by the activity of undersea volcanoes.

Quiz: If You . . .

1. If you bought something on the black market in Djibouti, in which country would you be running from the law—
Yemen or Saudi Arabia?

2. If you can visit the Island of Mull, the Island of Skye, and the Isle of Lewis, which country are you in—
Scotland or New Zealand?

3. If you are wandering in the Great Victoria Desert, which country are you in—
South Africa or Australia?

4. If you're determined to climb the Grossglocker, which country will you have to visit—
Austria or Germany?

5. If you're looking for Noah's Ark on Mount Ararat, which country will you have to go to—
Turkey or Iran?

6. If you were skiing in the Carpathian Mountains, which country would you be in—
Poland or the Czech Republic?

7. If you were standing on the Mosquito Coast, which country would you be in—
Ethiopia or Honduras?

8. If you're caught in the Turpan Depression, which country would you be in—
China or New Zealand?

9. If you've decided to travel the Khyber Pass, which two countries are you traveling through—
Afghanistan and Pakistan, or Turkey and India?

10. If you're standing at zero degrees latitude, where can you say you're standing—
on the North Pole or the equator?

ANSWERS

1. Yemen **2.** Scotland **3.** Australia **4.** Austria **5.** Turkey **6.** Czech Republic **7.** Honduras **8.** China **9.** Afghanistan and Pakistan **10.** Afghanistan and Pakistan

> The ancient cavern system of Ka'eleku Caverns at Hana on the Hawaiian island Maui, was created from hot molten lava flowing 30,000 years ago. Tourists can hike with experienced guides deep into the subterranean passages of one of the world's largest lava tubes.

The largest volcano known isn't on Earth, but on Mars: Olympus Mons is 370 miles wide and 79,000 feet high, nearly three times higher than Mount Everest.

> One of Jupiter's moons, Io, has active volcanoes.
> There are 40 active volcanoes in Alaska—more than in any other U.S. state.
> Italy's Mount Etna is still active and spewing lava.

In 1883, on August 27th, the greatest single volcanic explosion in the last 3,000 years was the eruption of Krakatoa in the Pacific. It was heard around the world. Tidal waves killed thousands, and the dust blasted into the atmosphere darkened the world's days for over two years.

> Wyoming's world-famous Devil's Tower, a nearly vertical monolith, rises 1,267 feet above the Belle Fourche River. Known by Northern Plains tribes as Bears Lodge, it is a sacred site of worship for many American Indians. Scientists are still undecided as to what exactly caused the natural wonder, although they agree that it is the remnant of volcanic activity.
> Iceland is the only northern European country where active volcanoes and hot springs can still be found.

Japan's Mount Fuji is actually a dormant volcano that last erupted in 1707.

> Spread for 200 miles, 24 active volcanoes are strung along Ecuador's Andean mountain range. Ecuador's volcanoes include Cotopaxi, Sangay, Reventador, Sumaco, and Pichincha. The Pan American Highway, which runs from the Colombian border south to Peru, is known as the Avenue of the Volcanoes.
> The world's tallest active volcano is the Guallatiri volcano in northern Chile. It stands 19,918 feet tall, and last erupted in 1987.
> Tourists who are eager to visit volcanoes that have recently erupted should take heed: volcanic ash has been known to remain hot for a period of nearly 100 years.

FOUR MOUNTS TO SURMOUNT

1. If you just climbed Mount Marra, you'd be in Sudan.

2. If you're on top of Mount Tahat, you'd be looking at Algeria.

3. If you're scaling Mount Boby, you've traveled to Madagascar.

4. If you've reached the summit of Mount Kenya, you've only ascended Africa's second-highest peak—Mount Kilimanjaro, in Kenya, is the first.

Course 774: **Only in America**

> Media mogul Ted Turner owns about 2 percent of New Mexico.
> About 250 million years ago, New York was part of a chain of volcanic islands, with an ocean on one side and a vast inland sea on the other.
> If you want to get technical, there are really only 46 states in the United States. The reason: Kentucky, Massachusetts, Pennsylvania, and Virginia are all commonwealths.
> North Carolina (not California) was the site of the first U.S. gold rush, which began in 1803. The state supplied all the domestic gold coined for currency by the U.S. Mint in Philadelphia until 1828.

The second national city is Port Angeles, Washington, as designated by President Abraham Lincoln. That's where he would have moved the capital if something happened to Washington, D.C.

> The United States today contains more than 100,000 mounds, earthworks, and fortifications that were built thousands of years ago by prehistoric people.
> Six of the 20-highest waterfalls in the world are in Yosemite National Park.
> Texas has 254 counties. Alaska, which is more than twice as large, hasn't any.

There are 61 towns in the United States with the word "turkey" in their names (Turkeytown, Alabama, and Turkey Foot, Florida, to name but two).

> In 1996, a Nevada panel designated the Las Vegas Strip a scenic byway, saying that the glitzy neon lights and erupting volcano, sinking pirate ship, pyramid, castle, and other casino attractions are culturally enriching.
> The state of Michigan claims more varieties of trees than all of Europe.
> According to legend, prospectors Ed Schieffelin and his brother Al were warned not to venture into the Apache-inhabited Mule Mountains because there they would only "find their tombstones." Thus, with a touch of the macabre, the Schieffelins named their first silver strike claim Tombstone, and it became the name of the Arizona town.
> The highest place people have settled in the United States is Climax, Colorado. It is at a height of 11,360 feet above sea level.

There are four places in the United States with the word *chicken* in their name: Chicken, Alaska; Chicken Bristle, in Illinois and Kentucky; and Chickentown, Pennsylvania.

> America's official national Christmas tree is located in King's Canyon National Park in California. The tree, a giant sequoia called the General Grant Tree, is over 90 meters (300 feet) high. It was made the official Christmas tree in 1925.
> The Capitol building in Washington, D.C., has 365 steps to represent every day of the year.
> Denver, Colorado, has 300 days of bright sunshine a year—more annual hours of sun than San Diego, California, or Miami Beach, Florida.

Chicago, Illinois, whose nickname is the Windy City actually has been ranked as only the 16th breeziest city in America.

> Missouri ("the Cave State") is home to more than 6,000 surveyed caves, including Meramec Caverns. Over the centuries, local tribes of Indians used the caverns as shelter. Local legend claims the caverns were used as a station on the Underground Railroad to hide escaping slaves. In the early 1870s, Jesse James and his band safely hid in the caverns after train and bank robberies.
> In North Carolina, where nearly 250,000 households likely still rely on primitive plumbing, state officials have announced a campaign to do away with outhouses.
> Not exactly in America, but—in New Zealand, the Presidential Highway links the towns of Gore and Clinton.

The Ku Klux Klan has applied to sponsor more than 16 miles of roadway under state adopt-a-highway programs. But will they only remove white trash?

GRAND FOLLY?

In January 2000, the U.S. Postal Service issued a Grand Canyon stamp. However, the photo used gave a mirror image of a view from the South Rim. The previous year, the Postal Service mistakenly labeled the Grand Canyon as a Colorado landmark on 100 million stamps. Those stamps were destroyed. One industry newspaper estimated the reprinting cost for the current mistake at $500,000, and so it was decided to distribute them with the reversed image.

Course 779: City Frights and Delights

> Australia's city of Sydney began as a penal colony in 1788; for the next 60 years, it received the criminal and persecuted people of British society.

> The first city to reach a population of 1 million people was Rome, Italy, in 133 B.C. London, England, followed in 1810, and New York City made it in 1875. Today, there are more than 300 cities in the world that boast a population in excess of 1 million.

The Italian city of Verona, where Shakespeare's Romeo and Juliet lived, receives about 1,000 letters addressed to Juliet every Valentine's Day.

> Built during the fourteenth century, Amsterdam's red-light district is an attractive part of the city, with charming architecture. The area originally was filled with houses of ill repute and many distilleries. The distilleries are gone, but the oldest of professions still flourishes.

> Dining on gourmet fare while rolling down the elegant shopping street of the Bahnhofstrasse in Zurich, Switzerland—by streetcar—is a common pleasure in the city. Called the Gastrotram, it's a favorite of the locals.

In the city of Reykjavik, Iceland, one can see the stars 18 hours a day during the heart of the winter. During the summer, sunlight is visible 24 hours a day. Reykjavik is likely the cleanest capital city in the world as well.

> The beautiful Antibes on the French Riviera is the luxury-yacht capital of the world. Antibes also hosts one of the largest antique shows in Europe each spring.

> In New York City there are more Irish than in Dublin, Ireland; more Italians, than in Rome, Italy; and more Jews than in Tel Aviv, Israel.

> According to a recent study, there are more than 100 art galleries in Scottsdale, Arizona, which surprisingly exceeds the number in either Los Angeles or San Francisco.

The nicknames of the famous marble lions that stand before the New York Public Library on Fifth Avenue have changed over the decades. But during the 1930s, Mayor Fiorello LaGuardia named them Patience and Fortitude—qualities he felt New Yorkers needed to survive the Depression. They are still so named.

STATE YOUR CITY!

The names of some cities in the United States are the names of other U.S. states. These include Nevada, Missouri; California, Maryland; Louisiana, Missouri; Oregon, Wisconsin; Kansas, Oklahoma; Wyoming, Ohio; Michigan, North Dakota; Indiana, Pennsylvania; and Delaware, Arkansas.

Final Exam

1. If one were to drive from Los Angeles, California, to Reno, Nevada, the direction in which he or she would be going is northwest.

True or False?

2. The Yucatán Peninsula, in Mexico, is the earliest documented place of human habitation in the Western Hemisphere.

True or False?

3. Old Faithful, the jewel of Yellowstone National Park, is not as dependable as it used to be.

True or False?

4. On March 27, 1964, North America's strongest recorded earthquake, with a magnitude of 9.2, rocked central California.

True or False?

5. Canada's east coast is closer to London than to its own west coast.

True or False?

6. Eskimos use wooden "eyeglasses" with narrow slits to protect their eyes from glare reflected by ice and snow.

True or False?

7. The South Pole gets almost exactly the same amount of rainfall as the Amazon jungle.

True or False?

8. The only U.S. state that is divided into two separate parts by a large body of water is Hawaii.

True or False?

9. The Himalayas are losing approximately 3 inches in height every year, and by the eleventh millennium (11,000 A.D.), they will no longer be the world's tallest mountain range.

True or False?

10. The cities of Montreal, Toronto, and Vancouver each have populations of over 1 million Canadian citizens.

True or False?

ANSWERS

1. TRUE.

2. FALSE. The earliest is Meadowcroft Rock Shelter in Washington County, Pennsylvania. Studies by anthropologist Dr. James Adovasio discovered evidence of early civilizations. Carbon dating revealed the remains were from human inhabitants living in the area 16,240 years ago.

3. TRUE. Because of vandalism and age-old geological shifts, the world's largest geyser is slowly losing its reputation for erupting like clockwork. In 1970, the average time between eruptions of the 126-year-old geyser was 66 minutes. The average today is about once every 77 minutes, or 18 times a day instead of 21. The geyser's power hasn't diminished, however.

4. FALSE. It rocked central Alaska. Each year Alaska has approximately 5,000 earthquakes, including 1,000 that measure above 3.5 on the Richter scale. Of the ten strongest earthquakes ever recorded in the world, three have occurred in Alaska.

5. TRUE.

6. TRUE.

7. FALSE. The South Pole is actually a desert environment, averaging about the same amount of monthly rainfall as the Sahara Desert.

8. FALSE. The state is Michigan.

9. FALSE. Actually, the Himalayas are the fastest-growing range on the planet. Their growth—about half an inch a year—is caused by the pressure exerted by two of Earth's continental plates (the Eurasian plate and the Indo-Australian plate) pushing against one another.

10. TRUE. Think we were trying to fool you!?

9

The USELESS
School of Film

Clearly, one of the problems with *Useful* Film Knowledge is that everyone else knows it as well, which is probably why no one is listening to you to begin with. Everyone already knows that Fred Astaire and Ginger Rogers were the greatest dance couple in movie history. But no one knows that their movie contracts forbade them to dance together in public. Everyone already knows that Jodie Foster starred in films like *Taxi Driver* and *Silence of the Lambs*. But few realize that she once exposed her butt to the whole country. When she was only three, Jodie was the bare-bottomed Coppertone tot in the famous print advertisement.

The evidence is solid: Useless Film Replacement Therapy is over 99 percent effective in removing all the years of movie sludge that have lodged in your cerebrum. For example, any synapses reserved for the film *Gladiator* can now be rejuvenated with the fact that, in his earlier acting years, the macho Russell Crowe played transvestite Dr. Frank N. Furter in a touring Australian stage production of *The Rocky Horror Picture Show*.

Speaking of *Rocky*, portions of the brain reserved for that film can also be erased and reprogrammed with the knowledge that when he was 15, Sylvester Stallone's high school chums voted him the one "most likely to end up in the electric chair." Even macho Brad Pitt had a yellow streak before becoming famous: he once held the position of a costumed chicken for an El Pollo Loco restaurant.

No matter what your age, height, weight, political agenda, or credit rating, remember this: Useless Film Knowledge has been shown to consume up to 47 times its weight in excess movie garbage that you can no longer stomach. So start rewriting all those scripts in your brain right now!

Course 304: **Before and After**

> At 17, Warren Beatty landed his first theater job—he became a rat catcher backstage at the National Theater in Washington.
> Before Albert Brooks became famous, he changed his name—from Albert Einstein. It seems that the father of relativity and the famous comedian both had the same name at birth.
> Before Gene Hackman and Dustin Hoffman catapulted to screen stardom in *The French Connection* and *The Graduate,* respectively, classmates at the Pasadena Playhouse voted them the two least likely to succeed.
> Early in his show business career, Richard Dreyfuss was in a Gleem toothpaste TV commercial.

Before *The Color Purple,* Whoopi Goldberg was a mortuary cosmetologist.

> Entertainers who worked in the pizza business before they became famous include Stephen Baldwin, Bill Murray, and Jean-Claude Van Damme.
> What do Warren Beatty, Uma Thurman, Sidney Poitier, Burt Reynolds, and Michael Caine have in common, besides being in the film business? Long before fame came their way, they worked as dishwashers.

> Early in his career, Jeff Daniels was in a Pepto Bismol TV ad.
> Kirk Douglas—who would later play a gladiator in *Spartacus*—was a wrestler in high school.

In the early 1950s, Clint Eastwood signed a $75-a-week contract with Universal to do walk-ons in low-budget horror flicks like *Revenge of the Creature*. He was fired when studio executives decided his Adam's apple protruded too much for him to be star material.

> Before *Superman* and *Popeye,* Christopher Reeve and Robin Williams were roommates at Juilliard.
> Former bouncers include Garth Brooks, John Goodman, Robert Mitchum, Oliver Reed, Burt Reynolds, Sylvester Stallone, and Jean-Claude Van Damme. Mickey Rourke was once a bouncer at a club for transvestites.
> Before he became a major film star, Errol Flynn worked as an inspector for a soft-drink company.
> In 1950, Sean Connery represented Scotland in London's Mr. Universe competition.

In 1972, Arnold Schwarzenegger appeared on TV's *The Dating Game.*

> Arrested for vagrancy as a teenager, Robert Mitchum served time on a Georgia chain gang.
> Charles Bronson and Jack Palance both labored as coal miners before they became successful in show business.
> Before directing *The Terminator* and *Titanic,* James Cameron drove trucks and school buses.

Before a wrist injury changed her career plans, legendary actress Marlene Dietrich had wanted to become a professional concert violinist.

> Jack Nicholson worked as an office boy in MGM's cartoon department before he was the Joker in *Batman*.
> George C. Scott—was a marine.
> Before beginning his movie career, Keanu Reeves managed a pasta shop in Toronto, Canada.

After high school graduation, Danny DeVito went to work in his sister's hair salon and was known to all her clients as Mr. Danny.

High Marx

On April 3, 1933, the Marx Brothers incorporated, choosing Harpo (known for being mute on screen) as president. Years later, the movie company Warner Bros.

threatened to sue Groucho Marx, leader of the famous comedy team, for giving his newest film the title *A Night in Casablanca* because it was too similar to their Bogart-Bergman film *Casablanca*. In his response, the acerbic Groucho growled back, "I'll sue you for using the word 'Brothers.'"

Course 311:
It's No Mickey Mouse Operation

> According to one source, Americans buy about 5 million items that are shaped like Mickey Mouse, or have a picture of Mickey Mouse on them, in the course of one day.

> According to the folks at Disney, there were 6,469,952 spots painted on the dogs in the original *101 Dalmatians*.

> In 1938, for his film *Snow White and the Seven Dwarves*, Walt Disney received a special honor—an Oscar and seven miniature statuettes.

Disney World in Orlando, Florida, covers 30,500 acres (46 square miles), making it twice the size of the island of Manhattan.

> Donald Duck comics were nearly banned years ago in Finland because Donald didn't wear pants.

> During World War I, young Walt Disney made money with another young man by painting helmets with camouflage colors, banging them up to look battle-scarred, and then selling them to Americans in search of realistic souvenirs.

> Harrison Ford is listed as one of 50 people barred from entering Tibet—apparently, Disney Studios clashed with Chinese officials over the film *Kundun* (1997).

H. R. Haldeman and Ron Ziegler, who helped plan the Watergate burglary for President Nixon, both worked at Disneyland when they were younger.

> Disneyland and Walt Disney World amusement parks are in counties with the same name. The former is in Orange County, California; the latter is in Orange County, Florida.

> The person in charge of polishing the brass poles in the Disneyland theme park spends six hours at the task every night.

When Walt Disney arrived in Hollywood in the early 1920s, he got a job as an extra in a Western movie. But it rained the day Walt's scene was to be filmed, and the studio replaced him.

HAIRY DECISION

In March 2000, the Disney company reversed its 43-year ban on mustaches for its theme-park employees. A memo sent to the 12,000 Disneyland and Walt Disney World employees said guests would be comfortable with "neatly trimmed mustaches." Founding father Walt Disney sported his own mustache, but that didn't stop him from banning facial hair in 1957. He took this action to distance his crew from stereotypical county-fair "carnies." The grooming code at the theme parks still bans beards, goatees, piercings, and unnatural hair colors.

Course 364: **Career Wonders and Blunders**

> Actors Robert Redford, Steve McQueen, and Paul Newman all turned down a contract offer of $4 million for the starring role in *Superman*. Little-known Christopher Reeve was paid $250,000 for the part.

> Actress Halle Berry turned down the role of Annie, and Stephen Baldwin turned down the role of Jack, in the 1994 *Speed*. The blockbuster film catapulted Sandra Bullock into stardom and greatly improved Keanu Reeve's box office appeal.

> Albert Finney turned down the role of Lawrence in David Lean's epic *Lawrence of Arabia* (1962). The part went to newcomer Peter O'Toole, who had not done a major film before. O'Toole's performance launched him to international fame.

The saga of O. J. Simpson has one more footnote, which has nothing to do with his Bruno Magli shoes. It was reported that director James Cameron desperately wanted O. J. to play the title role of the killer humanoid in his first *Terminator* film. Cameron held out for Simpson, but ended up settling for the then-little-known Arnold Schwarzenegger.

> Advised by his agent against taking on the part of Kid Shelleen in *Cat Ballou* (1965), Kirk Douglas turned it down. The role, that of a drunken gunfighter, went to Lee Marvin, who won his first Best Actor Oscar for his brilliant performance, as well as the Golden Globe Best Actor Award.

> Bert Lahr's unforgettable performance in *The Wizard of Oz* in 1939 apparently hurt his career in films. He told friend George Burns, "They call me every time a role comes up for a cowardly lion. Otherwise, they don't call me."

> Henry Fonda was originally offered the role of the TV newsman-gone-mad in *Network*, but turned it down.

Harrison Ford happily accepted a lead role passed over by Tom Selleck—that of archeologist Indiana Jones in *Raiders of the Lost Ark*.

> Bruce Willis declined the male lead in *Ghost* (1990), which costarred his then wife Demi Moore. Patrick Swayze took the part of the murdered man whose ghost remains on Earth.

> Charles Grodin was originally cast as Benjamin in *The Graduate* (1967), but the deal fell apart following a disagreement over his salary. Dustin Hoffman landed the lead role, which advanced his fledgling film career.

> Clint Eastwood was 41 years old when he debuted in *Dirty Harry* (1971). Reportedly, the part had been turned down by Paul Newman, John Wayne, Robert Mitchum, and Frank Sinatra.

James Dean was already to star in the 1956 film *Somebody Up There Likes Me* when his untimely death in a car accident sent studio bosses scrambling. After an exhaustive search, little-known actor Paul Newman was cast in the lead. Thus Dean's death actually helped Newman's film career come to life.

> As the Egyptian queen in *Cleopatra,* Elizabeth Taylor audaciously asked for, and received, the first $1 million contract in the film industry. The role was first offered to starlet Joan Collins, who turned it down.

> Frank Sinatra was first choice for the role of Jerry/Daphne in the comedy classic *Some Like It Hot* (1959). At the time, it was a risky role for any actor, as so much of it was played in drag. After much thought, Sinatra turned it down; Jack Lemmon happily accepted it, and film history was made. Lemmon received a Best Actor Golden Globe Award and an Oscar nomination for his delightful performance.

John Travolta refused starring roles in *Tootsie* and *An Officer and a Gentleman.*

> Meg Ryan turned down plum lead parts in the films *Steel Magnolias, Pretty Woman,* and *Silence of the Lambs*. A few years after her rejection of *Silence of the Lambs,* which earned Jodie Foster a Best Actress Oscar, Ryan disclosed to Barbara Walters in an interview that she had felt the role "was dangerous and a little ugly. I felt it was too dark—for me."

> The lead role of the television reporter in the film *The China Syndrome* (1979) was originally to be played by Richard Dreyfuss, but the character was changed to a woman—and Jane Fonda was cast in the part.

> In an interview, Sylvester Stallone remarked that he initially turned down the lead in *Romancing the Stone* (1984), which went to Michael Douglas. Instead, Stallone chose to star opposite Dolly Parton in the box-office flop *Rhinestone* (1984), about a country-and-western star who tries to turn a tone-deaf cabbie into a singer.

IN THE *NOT FUNNY* DEPARTMENT

Frank Sinatra was offered the male lead in the film *Funny Girl* (1968), but Barbara Streisand, who had performed the role successfully on Broadway, refused to take second billing, as did Sinatra. Even though this was her film debut, Streisand would not back down, and Sinatra, in a frustrated huff, dropped out. A deal with David Janssen to take the role fell apart. The part was ultimately given to the exotic Omar Shariff, on the heels of his success in *Doctor Zhivago*.

Seven Totally Psycho Facts!

1. Alfred Hitchcock bought the rights to the novel *Psycho* anonymously from author Robert Bloch for just $9,000. He then bought up as many copies of the novel as he could to keep the ending a secret.

2. During filming, this movie was referred to as "Production 9401" or "Wimpy."

3. Hitchcock used the crew from his TV series to save time and money on the film. The film only cost $800,000 to make, yet it has earned more than $40 million.

4. The actual house used for the design construction of the house in *Psycho* still stands in Kent, Ohio.

5. The shower scene has over 90 splices in it, and did not involve Anthony Perkins at all. Perkins was in New York preparing for a play.

6. The sound that the knife makes penetrating the flesh is actually the sound of a knife stabbing a casaba melon.

7. In the famous shower scene, chocolate syrup was used to simulate blood.

Course 363: **You're Not in Kansas**

> According to lead Munchkin Jerry Maren, the "little people" on the set of *The Wizard of Oz* (1939) were paid $50 per week for a six-day workweek, while Toto received $125 per week.
> During filming, Toto was stepped on by one of the witch's guards, and had a doggie double for two weeks.

The name of the magical land in Oz was created when author L. Frank Baum, struggling for the perfect name, looked at his filing cabinet and saw the labels "A–N" and "O–Z" on the drawers.

> L. Frank Baum, the author of the *The Wizard of Oz*, couldn't swim. He always smoked a cigar when he was wading in the water so that he could tell when he was getting in too deep.

> *The Wizard of Oz* was a Broadway musical 37 years before the MGM movie version was made. It had 293 performances and then went on a tour that lasted 9 years.
> In 1939, when she starred in *The Wizard of Oz,* actress Judy Garland was 16 years old.
> The most expensive pieces of movie memorabilia are the ruby slippers worn by Judy Garland in *The Wizard of Oz.* In May 2000, a pair of the slippers came up for auction at Christie's and brought in a winning bid of $666,000. The same pair was auctioned off in 1988, and brought in—a then record-breaking—$188,000.

TIME FOR YOUR MAKEUP!

It took one hour and 45 minutes each day to apply actor Jack Haley's silver-and-black makeup for his signature role as the Tin Man. Ray Bolger, as the Scarecrow, sat in the makeup chair for two hours. But Bert Lahr, the Cowardly Lion, had the worst time of it. Once his lion's mouth and nose prostheses were glued to his face, he couldn't even open his own mouth wide enough to chew. His lunch was whatever he could sip through a straw. His fur-covered lion costume, complete with fur mittens, was so heavy and hot that Lahr had to take the suit off completely after each shot, and each time it was dripping wet.

Course 394: **Not in the Script**

"If you can't do anything else, there's always acting."—Steve McQueen encouraging his karate teacher Chuck Norris to change careers

"I never go outside unless I look like Joan Crawford the movie star. If you want to see the girl next door, go next door."—Joan Crawford

"My friends know that to me happiness is when I am merely miserable and not suicidal."—Bob Fosse

If you have to tell them who you are, you aren't anybody."—Gregory Peck

"An actor's a guy who, if you ain't talking about him, ain't listening."—Marlon Brando

"If Bo Derek got the part of Helen Keller, she'd have trouble with the dialogue."—Joan Rivers

"She had something. She photographed well but of course, she copied me."—Mae West, commenting on Marilyn Monroe's death

"I don't want any yes-men around me. I want everybody to tell me the truth—even if it costs them their jobs."—producer Samuel Goldwyn

"If he'd have lived, they'd have discovered he wasn't a legend."—Humphrey Bogart on James Dean

"It is my intention to make no provision herein for my son Christopher or my daughter Christina for reasons which are well known to them."—from the will of Joan Crawford

"I had a video made of my recent knee operation. The doctor said it was the best movie I ever starred in."—Shirley Maclaine

"Acting is the most minor of gifts. After all, Shirley Temple could do it when she was four."—Katharine Hepburn

"I stopped believing in Santa Claus when I was six. Mother took me to see him in a department store, and he asked for my autograph."—Shirley Temple

> Critics raved over young Patty Duke's performance as Helen Keller in *The Miracle Worker*. When asked years later about all the acclaim, she answered, "I think the one that means the most was what my son Mack said after he saw the film when he was very little, maybe three or four. 'Mom,' he wanted to know, 'when did you get over being blind?'"

"If you become a star, you don't change, everyone else does."—Kirk Douglas

"I see my body just as a classy chassis to carry my mind around in."—Sylvester Stallone

During the making of the epic film *The Bible,* famous director John Huston lamented, "I don't know how God managed. I'm having a terrible time."

"The more time you have to think things through the more you have to screw it up."—Clint Eastwood on filmmaking

"Making movies is very complicated, tedious, and tiresome. It is especially terrible for a comic, because you do a joke and you turn to the people and ask, 'Was it funny?' They say, 'We'll let you know in eight months."—Arsenio Hall

"My problem lies with reconciling my gross habits with my net income."—Errol Flynn

Course 397: **Film History**

> The first film audiences in Hong Kong had to be paid to watch movies. The Chinese were frightened of the potential evil power of the "moving spirits" on the screen and refused to enter the theater.
> In the early days of silent movies, the British theater owner hired audiences by the day for three weeks, paying them for their attendance until their fears and superstitions were dispelled. The tactic paid off.

Grover Cleveland was the first U.S. president to star in a film. In 1895, the president was asked to appear in *A Capital Courtship,* and he agreed to be filmed while signing a bill into law.

> In the 1920s, cinema idol Rudolph Valentino was forced to take drastic security measures because fans continually invaded his home and pilfered his belongings as mementos. A 9-foot-high stucco wall and huge floodlights were erected at his mansion to keep female fans out. Additionally, three Great Danes, two Italian mastiffs, and one Spanish greyhound ran loose through the courtyard and terrace as sentries.

> The closest that film star John Wayne came to military action was in 1944 during a three-month entertainment tour of Pacific bases. His boyhood wish to become a naval officer never came true, though he did come close to receiving an appointment to Annapolis. During World War II, he was rejected for military service.

The nickname Tinsel Town was first coined by Oscar Levant, the pianist and composer, who observed: "Strip the phoney tinsel off Hollywood, and you'll find the real tinsel underneath."

> He starred in *It's a Wonderful Life,* but James Stewart was also a star in the military. In fact, the actor attained the highest U.S. service rank in history for an entertainer. After flying 20 missions over Germany as a bomber pilot during World War II, Stewart advanced from private to a full colonel and eventually rose to brigadier general in the U.S. Air Force Reserve.

> Marlene Dietrich was almost as famous for her sexual conquests as she was for her acting and singing. The immortal screen goddess was a bisexual beauty known for having slept with such legends as Frank Sinatra, Edith Piaf, Kirk Douglas, Adlai Stevenson, and even John F. Kennedy—whom Dietrich claimed to have bedded when she was 62.

> *The Manchurian Candidate,* with a full roster of stars headed by Frank Sinatra, hit theaters in 1962. Its subject matter, the attempted assassination of a president, was too close for comfort following the murder of John F. Kennedy. The film was pulled from circulation, and wasn't released from its vault for TV or VCR viewing for many years.

> During the 1950s, the average budget for a Three Stooges' film was about $16,000. This included the salaries of the three stars.

> Although the film had been banned in Afghanistan, *Titanic* fans in Kabul flocked to buy cosmetics, clothes, women's shoes, wedding cakes, cars, and even rice with connections to the movie. In the year 2000, 28 barbers in Kabul were arrested and jailed for copying Leonardo DiCaprio's hairstyle in the film. They were accused by Taliban courts of promoting hairdos which were anti-Islamic.

Titanic Coincidence?

Fourteen years before the *Titanic* sailed in April of 1912 on her maiden voyage from Southampton to New York, a novel entitled *Futility* was published. It was about an unsinkable and glamorous Atlantic liner, the largest in the world.

Like the *Titanic*, its passenger list was the crème de la crème, and there were not enough lifeboats on board. On a cold April night, the fictional "unsinkable" vessel strikes an iceberg and glides to the bottom of the Atlantic. The name of this liner, in the novella by Morgan Robertson, was *The Titan*.

> *True Lies*, starring Arnold Schwarzenegger, was attacked by Arab-Americans for its depiction of Middle Easterners as homicidal religious zealots. The American-Arab Anti-Discrimination Committee was one of four groups protesting at a Washington theater when the film opened; a boycott of the movie was called. Despite the boycott and the controversy, the film was one of the top moneymakers of 1994, earning more than $150 million.

A lament from bestselling author John LeCarré on the nature of filmmaking: "Having your book turned into a movie is like seeing your oxen turned into bouillon cubes."

> After U.S. warplanes accidently bombed their embassy in Yugoslavia in May 1999, the Chinese government temporarily yanked U.S. movies from its theaters. *Saving Private Ryan* was replaced with films from the 1950s showing Chinese soldiers bravely fighting U.S. troops during the Korean War.
> The film *Anna and the King* (1999), like its predecessor *The King and I*, was banned from Thai movie houses. Censors ruled that the movie, starring Jodie Foster as Victorian governess Anna Leonowens and Hong Kong's Chow Yun-Fat as the king of Siam (now Thailand), paid insufficient respect to the royal family.

Course 396: **Odds and Ends**

> Lauren Bacall's singing was dubbed in the film *To Have and Have Not* (1944). But because her speaking voice was so low, it was impossible to find a female singer who could match her voice satisfactorily, so she was eventually dubbed by a guy—Mel Torme.
> Think it was Diane Keaton who made her film debut in Woody Allen's *Annie Hall*? Think again—it was Sigourney Weaver.

At director Martin Scorsese's request, actor Joe Pesci wrote and directed the "You think I'm funny?" scene in the film *Goodfellas* (1990).

> Dooley Wilson appeared as Sam in the movie *Casablanca*. Wilson was a drummer—not a pianist—in real life. The man who really played the piano

in *Casablanca* was a Warner Bros. staff musician who was at the keys off camera during the filming.

> The first French kiss in a general-release U.S. film took place between Warren Beatty and Natalie Wood, in *Splendor in the Grass*.
> In *Saturday Night Fever* (1977), rising star John Travolta wanted his disco suit to be black, but he would have literally disappeared against his female costar's red dress. So Travolta wore his soon-to-be famous white disco suit, which sold for $145,000 in 1995.
> Thirty-two writers worked on the screenplay for the 1994 film The Flintstones.

In *Star Wars* (1977), what appear at the end of the film to be hundreds of people watching the heroes receive their medallions from Princess Leia are mostly cardboard cutouts.

> The 1988 blockbuster movie *Titanic* lasts 3 hours and 14 minutes. The actual ship took 2 hours and 40 minutes to sink after hitting an iceberg.
> In a 1996 interview, comedian Jerry Lewis claimed that he was among the first to spot young Steven Spielberg's talent. He showed Spielberg's short film *Amblin* to his University of Southern California class, which included students George Lucas and Francis Ford Coppola.
> Reportedly, film comedian W.C. Fields drank two quarts of martinis a day, even when working on the set. In his final years, he suffered from cirrhosis and kidney trouble, and had to wear heavy makeup in his last films to conceal the swollen veins and "gin blossoms" on his face and nose.
> American director Orson Welles is buried in an olive orchard on a ranch owned by a friend, matador Antonio Ordonez, in Sevilla, Spain.

Actor John Barrymore had a pet vulture named Maloney that would sit on his knee and hiss.

> We all know that Charles Foster Kane's sled was named Rosebud. But he really had two sleds in *Citizen Kane*—the other was named Crusader.
> Hollywood actress Joan Crawford had her back teeth removed to make her cheekbones more prominent.

India, not the United States, is the number-one movie producer in the world. Annually, India averages more than 800 films, compared to just over 500 in the States. In fact, India's thriving film industry has been nicknamed Bollywood, since the bulk of the business is based in Bombay.

> The Chateau Marmont—located in the heart of Hollywood—is so trendy that instead of putting Bibles on the nightstands in its suites, it provides guests with screenplays.
> The last line of the movie *Easy Rider* was "We blew it!"

Dustin Hoffman, as Tootsie, wore a size 36C bra.

Final Exam

1. Before his career as a movie superstar, Arnold Schwarzenegger, even though he held a record number of bodybuilding championship titles, was usually broke. Once he had to borrow money from a girlfriend to fly back to his home in Los Angeles from Chicago.

True or False?

2. When George Burns died less than two months after celebrating his 100th birthday in 1996, relatives honored his request that he be buried in a crypt on top of his wife and long-time comedy-act partner, Gracie Allen, because he wanted to eternally preserve his "top billing."

True or False?

3. Rubber-faced Jim Carrey portrayed the late great comedian Andy Kaufman in the film *Man on the Moon*, and the two also shared the same birthday—January 17th.

True or False?

4. Edda van Heemstra, born in Belgium, changed her name to Katharine Hepburn.

True or False?

5. Alfred Hitchcock, famed director of films such as *Psycho* and *The Birds*, suffered his entire life from a peculiar fear of eggs.

True or False?

6. Bruce Willis, Bette Midler, George Clooney, and John Ritter were all elected and served as the class presidents of their high school student councils.

True or False?

7. Actor Leslie Nielsen grew up 200 miles south of Miami on the lush island of Antigua.

True or False?

8. Before filming the role of Iris, the teen prostitute in the 1976 film *Taxi Driver*, actress Jodie Foster had to undergo extensive liposuction.

True or False?

9. Before tackling *Coming Home*, Jon Voight spent 11 weeks at the Rancho Los Amigos Hospital near Los Angeles interviewing 500 paraplegics to find out how they conducted sexual relations.

True or False?

10. Actress Rita Moreno is listed in the *Guinness Book of World Records* as the first actress to win over $1,000,000 in the California State Lottery.

True or False?

ANSWERS

1. FALSE. Schwarzenegger holds a degree in business and finance from the University of Wisconsin, and had earned a small fortune in mail order and real estate before he launched his career in the film industry.

2. FALSE. He was buried *beneath* her, because he wanted to finally let *her* have TOP billing!

3. TRUE. In the biographical film *Man on the Moon* (1999), the role of young Carol Kaufman, Andy Kaufman's sister, was played by Andy's real-life granddaughter Brittany Colonna.

4. FALSE. She changed it to Audrey Hepburn.

5. TRUE. According to his biographer Donald Spoto, Alfred Hitchcock had other peculiar fears as well, including acute anxiety whenever he saw a policeman coming his way.

6. TRUE.

7. FALSE. He grew up in a log cabin 200 miles south of the Arctic Circle.

8. FALSE. She had to undergo psychiatric evaluation by the California Labor Board. Because Jodie was a minor, the board had to determine if she was capable of handling the controversial role.

9. TRUE.

10. FALSE. Rita was the first performer to win the four major awards of film, music, TV, and theater (an Oscar, Grammy, Emmy, and Tony).

10

The USELESS
School of
Culinary Arts

Are you hungering to learn the most intricate secrets of the finest gourmets? Well, you've come to the wrong place. However, next time someone tries to force you to consume some home fries, simply refuse on religious grounds, citing as evidence the fact that the Scots for hundreds of years refused to eat potatoes because they weren't mentioned in the Bible.

Sushi anyone? Well, as your dinner companions are agonizing over the issue of salmon teriaki versus the California roll, you can drop a tidbit of information almost no Westerner knows—that Japanese chopsticks are pointed at the eating end and Chinese chopsticks are blunt. Continue to astound them by asking the waiter for "sake-mizu." The waiter will smile as you patiently explain to your comrades that the word *sake* (Japanese wine made from fermented rice) is shortened from the word *sake-mizu*, which translates as "prosperous waters," in case they didn't know.

Even your snobbiest food friends can be rightfully shamed, especially when it comes to French wine. Lecture them that in the 1980s and early 1990s, the French wine industry was plagued with bad corks. These gave many wines a moldy, damp-basement smell and taste. But the nastiness was not exclusively the fault of the corks. It also came from insecticides in the new wood used when many French wineries renovated their cellars in the prosperous 1980s. Fumes from insecticide-permeated wood found their way into the barrels and tanks of maturing wine.

Then—as they wipe their brows in awe—order a California merlot. Say that it was personally recommended to you by famed chef Wolfgang Puck, who (as you're sure all your dinner pals already know) chose the name Spago for his popular restaurants because in Italian *spago* means "string" or "twine," which is slang for spaghetti.

Yes, sir, there is nothing like Useless Food Knowledge to make other people immediately lose their appetite. So start digesting the following courses as quickly as possible!

Course 901: **History in Small Bites**

> A twelfth-century Egyptian rabbi was the first to prescribe soup made from a fat hen for colds.

> *Big cheese* and *big wheel* were medieval terms of envious respect for those who could afford to buy whole wheels of cheese at a time—an expense few could enjoy. Both terms are often used sarcastically today.

> In the U.S. Colonial period, salmon was quite plentiful and cheap on the Atlantic coast. Back then, some servants stipulated in their work contracts that they would not be served salmon at a meal more than once a week.

Honey is the only food that does not spoil. Honey found in the tombs of Egyptian pharaohs has been tasted by archaeologists and found edible.

> Beef seems so American, but it was actually an import. In the sixteenth century, Spaniards brought the first cattle to what would become the United

States. Originally, the settlers regarded them as beasts of burden, but the Indians found them delicious. The Indians, in fact, were the first cattle herders, and they were the ones who moved the cattle across the Mississippi River to the grasslands of the plains.

> Chewing gum reached the United States in the late 1800s when the exiled Santa Anna came to New York after a revolution in Mexico, bringing *chicle* (gum) with him. *Chicle* is a gum taken from the sapodilla tree, which grows in the Yucatán desert of Mexico.

French fries did not originate in France; it is believed that they started in Belgium and spread to France.

> Some historians say the origins of the tamale date to the pre-Columbian period in Mexico. They believe Aztecs and Mayans developed it as a convenient way to bring food to battlefronts.

> During the Alaskan Klondike gold rush (1897–98), potatoes were practically worth their weight in gold. They were so valued for their vitamin C content that miners traded gold for them.

Frozen foods were created in the mid-1920s by Clarence Birdseye. While doing survey work for the U.S. government in Labrador in 1912, he observed the natives preserving their fish in ice, and expanded on the concept.

> Ellis Island immigrants were often served a bowl of Jell-O as a welcome to America.

> In Middle Eastern legend, the banana was widely considered to be the forbidden fruit.

MY! MY! WHAT A PIE!!

Centuries back, the wealthy English were known for the surprise pie. This odd culinary creation was a main dish, and was brought to the banquet table with great fanfare. It was opened ceremoniously, and out of the pie leaped all sorts of live creatures: frogs, squirrels, terriers, foxes, and as the nursery rhyme claims, four-and-twenty blackbirds. At one grand party, a dueling dwarf reportedly popped out and cavorted on top of the banquet table.

The serving of surprise pies was a gala affair for years, until Oliver Cromwell came into power. He banned the eating of pie in 1644, declaring it a pagan form of pleasure. For 16 years, pie making and pie eating went underground. In 1660, the Restoration leaders lifted the ban on pie.

Course 910: **Hard to Swallow**

> Flamingo tongues were thought to be a delicacy by ancient Romans.
> The Romans were so fond of eating doormice that the upper classes raised them domestically in specially designed cages. In ancient China and certain parts of India as well, mouse flesh was considered a marvelous delicacy. In ancient Greece, where the mouse was sacred to Apollo, mice were eagerly devoured by temple priests.

A popular Samoan dish is baked bat. First the bat is torched to "de-hair" it. It is cleaned, and then baked or fried with salt, pepper, and onions.

> A Zanzibari delicacy is white ant pie. White termites are combined with sugar and banana flour and mixed into a paste.
> Chicken feet are an extremely popular dim sum dish in Asia. Not surprisingly, they aren't popular with Americans. They are prepared simply in a black-bean sauce. The proper way to eat them is to put the entire chicken's foot in one's mouth, suck off the meat, and spit out the bones.

According to the U.S. Food and Drug Administration, peanut butter will meet federal safety standards if it contains up to 210 insect fragments per 700 grams, an average-size jar of peanut butter. Additionally, that same jar may contain up to 7 whole rodent hairs before being considered unsanitary.

> Alligator meat is usually only available for sale in its native regions of Louisiana and the Gulf States in the United States. Alligator comes in three basic types: the preferred tender, veal-like tail meat; the pinkish body meat, which has a stronger flavor and slightly tougher texture; and the dark tail meat, which is best when used in braised dishes.

The unusual, but popular, French dish "beef udder pot roast" is comprised of a cow's mammaries that have been simmered with vegetables in beef stock.

> Two of the more unusual and popular dishes in Ecuador are roasted *cuy,* or guinea pig, and *tronquito,* which is bull penis soup.
> Haggis, a traditional Scottish dish, is made from the lungs, heart, and liver of a sheep, chopped with onions, seasonings, suet, and oatmeal, and then broiled in a bag made from the sheep's stomach.
> British Airways tested ostrich meat on first-class passengers in 1996. Because they are a low-cholesterol alternative to beef, and because of Britain's "mad cow disease" plague, ostrich steaks were viewed as a healthy dish. The bird premiered as the "Chef's Special" on London–New York City flights.

Korea's *poshintang*—dog meat soup—is a popular item on summertime menus. The soup is believed to cure summer heat ailments and improve virility and women's complexions.

> Official FDA guidelines allow whole pepper to be sold with up to 1 percent of the volume made up of rodent droppings.

A person who is lost in the woods and starving can obtain nourishment by chewing on his or her shoes. Leather has enough nutritional value to sustain life for a short time. Talk about polishing off a meal!

Water on the Brain

The average American consumes 1,500 pounds of food each year. 1,000 gallons of water are required to grow and process each pound of that food. This means that in the United States, in a single year, an average of 1.5 million gallons of water are invested in the food eaten by just one person. This 200,000-cubic-feet-plus of water per-person would be enough to cover a football field 4 feet deep. Of course, that doesn't include the water used flushing the toilet.

Course 921: Chocolate Without Fudging

> In a survey conducted by a women's magazine, 70 percent of female respondents said they would rather have chocolate than sex, according to the Chocolate Manufacturers Association.
> Chocolate contains the same chemical, phenylethylamine, that your brain produces when you fall in love. But don't have too much—an excess of phenylethylamine makes people very nervous.
> Chocolate was adored by Montezuma, emperor of the Aztecs. In the early 1500s, he drank as much as 50 glasses of chocolate every day.

A favorite dish of the Aztecs was roast turkey with chocolate gravy. Hernando Cortez, the Spanish conquistador, brought the drink back to Spain in 1529. It remained a favorite of Spanish royalty for many years before becoming popular throughout Europe.

> Drinking chocolate mixed with milk, wine, or beer was considered a must at fashionable social events in the seventeenth century.

In France, chocolate was initially met with skepticism and was considered a barbarous, noxious drug. The French court accepted chocolate after the Paris faculty of medicine gave its approval for consuming it.

> Quakers sang the praises of chocolate drinks as a healthful substitute for gin in the early 1700s.
> Milk chocolate was introduced in 1875, when Henry Nestlé, a maker of evaporated milk, and Daniel Peter, a chocolate manufacturer, got together and invented it.

First Lady Eleanor Roosevelt ate three chocolate-covered garlic balls every morning. Her doctor recommended this to improve her memory.

> The biggest Hershey's Kiss ever fashioned weighed 400 pounds. It was specially made as a promotion to let the people of Hong Kong know about Hershey's products.
> Black chocolate contains caffeine—white chocolate does not.

Chocolate can be lethal to dogs. Theobromine, an ingredient that stimulates the cardiac muscle and the central nervous system, causes chocolate's toxicity. As little as 2 ounces of milk chocolate can be poisonous for a 10-pound puppy.

Course 930: **Perk Up**

> James Mason (not the film actor) patented the coffee percolator in 1865.
> The coffee filter was invented by Melitta Bentz in Germany in 1908. She pierced holes in a tin container, put a circular piece of absorbent paper in the bottom of it, and put her creation over a coffeepot.
> According to Dr. Bruce Ames of the University of California at Berkeley, there are more than 1,000 chemicals in a cup of coffee. Of these, only 26 have been tested, and half caused cancer in rats.
> According to the National Safety Council, coffee is not successful at sobering up a drunk person, and in many cases it may actually increase the adverse effects of alcohol.

Centuries ago, men were told the evil effects of coffee would make them sterile; women were cautioned to avoid caffeine unless they wanted to be barren.

> In Turkey, in the sixteenth and seventeenth centuries, anyone caught drinking coffee was put to death.

> Coffee beans are not beans, but the pits of a fruit that resemble beans. But no matter what they are, approximately 2,000 of them are needed to make one pound of coffee.

> Red-eye gravy is composed of ham drippings and coffee. Its heavier ingredients settle in the bottom of the bowl in the shape of a red eye, giving the gravy its name.

> Hawaii is the only U.S. state that produces coffee.

> The Swedes drink more coffee than any other people in the world.

> The bubbles in coffee can foretell what the day's weather will be. Stare at your coffee before adding milk. If the bubbles float toward the rim of the cup, the pressure is low, and clouds and stormy weather can be expected. However, if the bubbles float to the center, the pressure is high, and fair weather can be expected.

Ulcers seem to be aggravated more by decaffeinated coffee than by regular coffee, according to the Center for Ulcer Research and Education in California.

> The world's rarest coffee comes from Indonesia. At approximately $300 U.S. dollars per pound, *kopi luwak* is the end product (get the picture) of a catlike marsupial, called the paradoxurus, that loves eating coffee beans. The enzymes in the animal's stomach add a unique flavor, and the beans are only collected after they are excreted.

> The origin of coffee can be traced back to East Africa. Legend has it that an Ethiopian shepherd noticed that his sheep stayed awake all night after grazing on coffee beans. When the shepherd ate them, they had the same effect on him.

In Saudi Arabia, a woman reportedly may divorce her husband if he does not keep her supplied with coffee.

BACH AGAINST THE WALL

Frederick the Great of Prussia wanted to make coffee off-limits to his subjects because of the huge sums of money that were going to foreign exporters. "My people must drink beer," Frederick demanded in a manifesto. Rumors flew furiously, including one that claimed coffee made people sterile.

But composer Johann Sebastian Bach disagreed vehemently with Frederick and his anticoffee crowd. So in retaliation, he wrote the *Coffee Cantata*, published in 1732. It told the story of a father who threatens to break off his daughter's marriage plans unless she gives up her vile coffee-drinking habit. The girl agrees, but changes her mind when her mother and grandmother reveal that they have always been passionate, although secretive, coffee drinkers (and obviously not infertile). Bach himself was the father of 20 children.

Course 944: **All in the Family**

> Apples are a member of the rose family—and so are pears.
> Asparagus is a member of the lily family. The name *asparagus* comes from Greek and means "sprout" or "shoot."
> Lettuce is a member of the sunflower family.
> Botanically speaking, true members of the berry family include the grape, tomato, and eggplant, but not raspberries and blackberries.

A tomato is a fruit, but it is legally known as a vegetable. In 1893, there was a case before the U.S. Supreme Court about importing tomatoes from the West Indies. Fruits could be imported tax-free, but vegetables couldn't. Since tomatoes were eaten with main dishes and not as or with desserts, the Court ruled them to be a vegetable.

> Baby-cut carrots aren't baby carrots. They're actually full-sized ones peeled and polished down to size. And there's nothing small about their current popularity: about 25 percent of California's fresh carrot crop is turned into babies.
> A peanut is not a nut; it is part of the legume family.

The cashew nut is a member of the poison ivy family.

> Post Grape-Nuts cereal does not contain grapes or even nuts; it is made from natural wheat and barley. This unique, naturally sweet cereal was created in 1897 by C. W. Post, who named it Grape-Nuts: "Grape" because it contained maltose, which C. W. called "grape sugar," and "Nuts" because of its flavor.

Course 969: **Hazardous to Your Health—or Not?**

> Believe it or not, hors d'oeuvres can be dangerous. Many people die each year swallowing the toothpicks of hors d'oeuvres.
> When potatoes first appeared in Europe in the seventeenth century, it was thought that they were disgusting, and they were blamed for starting outbreaks of syphilis. As late as 1720 in America, eating potatoes was believed to shorten a person's life.
> Nearly two centuries later, potatoes were banned in Burgundy in 1910 because it was believed "frequent use caused leprosy."

Drugs taken with grapefruit juice may be absorbed by the body more easily. Which means people who drink great quantities of grapefruit juice with their pills can make themselves gravely ill.

> More people are allergic to cow's milk than to any other food.

Virtually one-third of all the bottled drinking water bought in America is contaminated with bacteria.

> The body won't absorb the calcium from milk if it's drunk in the same meal as meat. There needs to be at least 2 hours between milk and meat intake for best results. Sounds kosher to us.

> A traditional drink found throughout Andean countries is *chicha,* made from fermented maize or rice. The fermentation process is augmented by human saliva in some rural parts of Ecuador. *Chicha* makers, usually women, chew the ingredients and then spit them back in the pot to brew. Visitors should avoid sampling the brew, as hepatitis B is commonly passed in this way.

SPEAKING OF FOOD ADDITIVES

Many of the foods in Victorian England had poisons added to them for purely aesthetic purposes. To heighten color, excessive chalk was put in milk, and sulfate of copper was put in pickles. Butter, bread, and most of the gin consumed had copper added to them. Red lead gave Gloucester cheese its red hue. Lead became an ingredient of wine, cider, and chocolate as well. With the accumulative effect, the result was often chronic gastritis and fatal food poisoning for many thousands of Brits.

Course 973: **Very Intoxicating**

> Circa 1116 B.C., a Chinese imperial edict claimed that the use of alcohol in moderation was required by heaven.

> The word *toast,* meaning a proposal of health, originated in Rome, where an actual bit of spiced, burned bread was dropped into wine to improve the drink's flavor, absorb its sediment, and thus make it more healthful.

> The first beer brewed in England was made by the Picts about 250 B.C. It was made from heather and probably had hallucinogenic effects.

In olden times, saloons offered free lunches, most of which were overly salted, forcing the diner to buy a drink. Hence the phrase: there's no such thing as a free lunch.

> In English pubs, ale is ordered by pints and quarts. In old England, when customers became unruly, the bartender would yell at them to mind their own "pints and quarts" and settle down. Legend has it that's where we got the abbreviated phrase "mind your p's and q's."

> The Greek god of wine was Dionysus. St. Amand of Maastricht is the patron saint of beer and wine sellers.

A *punt* is the conical indentation at the bottom of a wine bottle. Its purpose is to strengthen the structure of the bottle and to trap the sediments in the wine.

> It takes the same amount of time to age a cigar as to age wine.
> Surprisingly, about 93 percent of households in Denmark consume wine, the highest consumption rate of any country. French homes follow with about 85 percent.

The phrase *wet your whistle* comes from old England, where whistles were baked into the rims or handles of ceramic cups used in pubs. When the customer needed a refill, he blew the whistle to summon the waiter.

TALES OF COCKTAILS

The term *cocktail* was invented in Elmsford, New York. A barmaid named Betsy Flanagan reportedly decorated her establishment with the tail feathers of cocks. One day a patron asked for "one of those cock tails." She served him a drink with a feather in it.

The Mai Tai cocktail, made with dark rum and orange curacao, was created in 1945 by Victor Bergeron, also known as Trader Vic. The drink got its name when he served it to two friends from Tahiti, who exclaimed "Maitai roa ae!" In Tahitian, the phrase means "out of this world"—the best!

The Manhattan cocktail—whiskey and sweet vermouth—was invented by Jennie Jerome, the beautiful New York socialite who was the toast of the town until she went to England as the wife of Lord Randolph Churchill in 1874. She later gave birth to baby Winston Churchill. The rest is history.

> Beer was not sold in bottles until 1850. Before then, a person went to the local tavern with a bucket or a pot made specially for holding beer, had it filled, and then carried it home.
> Beer was the catalyst in the first paving of an American street. Stone Street in New York was paved so that the city's beer wagons could easily get through the watery muck from the breweries.

The age recorded on a whiskey bottle refers to the number of years it is aged prior to being bottled. Once in the bottle, whiskey does not improve.

> *Mead,* a wine made from honey, is the national drink of Poland.

The California Board of Equalization has ruled that bartenders cannot be held responsible for misjudging the age of midgets.

The nickname of Mary I, Queen of England from 1553–1558, was Bloody Mary because of her notorious, violent persecution of Protestants. The Bloody Mary, a vodka-and-tomato-juice drink, was named after her.

When blind cellar master Dom Perignon discovered champagne back in 1668, he called out in ecstasy, "Oh, come quickly. I am drinking the stars."

FLASH! RISING SUN SEES RED

In Japan, a gruesome TV drama series, *Shitsurakuen* (or, *Paradise Lost*), popularized the drinking of red wine. The Japanese demand for red wine exploded when the show's main characters committed suicide by mixing poison with Chateau Margaux. Many Japanese wine drinkers switched from the preferred white to red after the 1997 TV episode aired. Advertising agencies said the macabre show pushed up not only red wine sales but wineglass sales as well.

Course 993: **How Sweet It Is!**

> Ice cream was invented in China around 2000 B.C. when the Chinese packed a soft milk-and-rice mixture in snow.

> About A.D. 62, the Roman emperor Nero sent slaves to the tops of the Apennine Mountains to bring fresh snow down to the royal kitchens, where the snow was then flavored with fruits and honey.

> After more than a century as a dessert for royalty alone, ice cream was made available to the general public for the first time at Café Procope, the first café in Paris, in 1670.

> Baskin-Robbins introduced the flavor Lunar Cheesecake to commemorate America's landing on the moon on July 20, 1969.

> Hershey's Kisses went out of production during World War II because the silver used to wrap them in was necessary for the war efforts. A special candy bar was produced for troops in the field.

The Baby Ruth candy bar was not named after the legendary Babe Ruth. It was actually named after Grover Cleveland's baby daughter, Ruth.

> Biscotti, a popular biscuit in hip coffeehouses that is baked twice and resistant to mold, was part of Christopher Columbus's food supply when he set out on his long voyages.

> Jell-O is made of hydrolyzed collagen, which is partially decomposed protein taken from cow and pig hides, hooves, bones, and connective tissue. The

protein in these animal materials is broken down with an alkaline solution and then extracted with hot water.

> The first chocolate chip cookie was developed in the kitchen of a Whitman, Massachusetts, country inn in 1937. Experiments led to a recipe combining bits of chocolate candy with a shortbread type cookie dough.

If all the Oreo cookies sold to date were stacked on top of each other, the height of the stack would be equivalent to the height of 9.8 million Sears Towers. The sears Tower is 1,454 feet tall.

> First manufactured in 1930, the Snickers Bar is the number-one-selling candy bar in the United States.
> As the official taste tester for Eddy's Grand Ice Cream, John Harrison had his taste buds insured for $1 million.

The names of the six Gummi bears are Gruffi, Cubbi, Tummi, Zummi, Sunni, and Grammi.

Where's the Beef?

When McDonald's wanted to open restaurants in India, it had to eliminate the portion of its menu that Americans equate with the fast-food giant: hamburgers. Hindus, who make up a large portion of India's population, consider the cow a sacred animal and its slaughter a sacrilege. And Muslims shun pork. So Indian customers at McDonald's can instead order a Maharaja Mac—two all-lamb patties.

Course 987:
Great Moments in Edible History

> The Caesar salad is not named after Julius Caesar. It is named for its creator, Caesar Cardini, who first prepared the salad in his Caesar's Palace Restaurant in Tijuana, Mexico.
> Philadelphia druggist Townsend Speakman invented the world's first soda pop in 1807. The drink consisted of carbonated water mixed with fruit flavors, and was called a nephite julep.
> The ice-cream soda was invented in 1874, when Robert N. Green ran out of cream for drinks made with cream, flavored syrup, and soda water. Green substituted ice cream, and the ice-cream soda was born.

> At the St. Louis World's Fair in 1904, Richard Blechyden, an Englishman, had a tea concession. On a very hot day, none of the fair goers were interested in drinking hot tea. Blechyden served the tea cold—and invented iced tea.

In 1889, Aunt Jemima pancake flour, invented at St. Joseph, Missouri, became the first self-rising flour for pancakes and the first ready-mix food ever to be introduced commercially.

> Denver, Colorado, lays claim to the invention of the cheeseburger. The trademark for the name "cheeseburger" was awarded in 1935 to Louis Ballast of the Humpty Dumpty Drive-In. Ballast claimed to have come up with the idea while testing hamburger toppings.
> PEZ Candy was first marketed as a compressed peppermint candy over 70 years ago in Vienna, Austria. The name PEZ was derived from the German word for "peppermint"…*PfeffErminZ*. Today, more than 3 billion PEZ candies are consumed annually in the United States alone.
> In 1945, Percy Spencer discovered that when popcorn was placed under microwave energy, it popped. This led to many experiments with other foods, and ultimately, to the birth of the microwave oven.

The Smithsonian Institute held its first (and only) conference on the history of Jell-O in 1991. Presentation titles included "The Dialectics of Jell-O in Peasant Culture," "American History Is Jell-O History," and "Jell-O Food Wrestling." There was also an exciting Jell-O Jell-Off Cooking Contest.

FROZEN IN TIME

Swanson executive Gerry Thomas came up with the idea of frozen dinners to get rid of 520,000 pounds of the company's excess turkey. In the early 1950s, Thomas sketched a drawing of a three-compartment aluminum tray, presented it to the Swansons—his bosses—and came up with the name "TV dinner." The first TV dinner meal consisted of turkey, corn bread dressing and gravy, buttered peas, and sweet potatoes. It sold for 98 cents (or about $6 in today's money). Although initially the company timidly ordered only 5,000 TV dinners, the Swanson company sold 10 million the first year.

Course 982: Soft Drinks—the Hard Facts!

> The original name of Pepsi-Cola was Brad's Drink.
> Lithiated Lemon was the creation of Charles Griggs from Missouri, who introduced the lemon-lime drink in 1929. Four years later, he renamed it 7-Up. Sales increased significantly.

Because of the political-contribution habits of the two soft-drink companies, Democratic administrations traditionally serve Coca-Cola and Republican administrations serve Pepsi.

> The United States is second in Coca-Cola consumption, with 395 servings of their soft drinks, including Sprite, ingested per person each year. In first place is Mexico, where each person drinks 412 servings per year.
> Coca-Cola was originally billed as an "esteemed brain tonic and intellectual beverage" when it first appeared on the market in 1886.
> Pepsi-Cola's advertising slogan in 1903 was "Exhilarating, Invigorating, Aids Digestion."

Pepsi's slogan "Come alive with the Pepsi Generation" translated onto Taiwan's billboards as "Pepsi brings your ancestors back from the dead."

> Laverne De Fazio's favorite drink in the TV series *Laverne and Shirley* was Pepsi and milk.
> President Lyndon Johnson was apparently so fond of Fresca that he had a special fountain installed in the Oval Office that dispensed the beverage. It could be operated by the president pushing a button on his desk chair.

Waco, Texas, famous for the deadly fate of the Branch-Davidian compound, is slightly less well-known as the birthplace of Dr Pepper soda.

> Most common sports drinks are the equivalent of sugar-sweetened human sweat. That is, they have the same salt concentration as sweat (but are less salty than your blood). An increase of as little as 1 percent in blood salt will cause you to become thirsty.

The official soft drink of the cool state of Nebraska is Kool-Aid.

Course 989: **Eat These Words**

> A diet of bread and water is called *xerophagy*.

***Mageiricophobia* is the intense and paralyzing fear of having to cook.**

> A small or imperfect ear of corn is called a *nubbin*.
> A literal translation of the word *wonton* is "swallowing a cloud." Wontons floating in soup often resemble tiny clouds.

SPAM is an acronym formed from two words: spiced ham.

> The phrase *fortified with iron* means there are actually pieces of metal in your cereal. If you ran a powerful magnet through fortified cereal, tiny black specks of iron would appear on the flakes. Don't worry, the body needs iron, and this is a good way to get it.
> Milk that has become thicker due to becoming sour is referred to as *bonnyclabber.*

Pumpernickel bread is thought to be named for the German words meaning "devil fart." In German, *pumpern* means "to fart," and *Nickel* means "devil, demon, or goblin." Supposedly the bread causes gas as powerful as that which the Devil experiences.

> Oh, yes, the glue on Israeli postage stamps is certified kosher.

DON'T GET PANNED IN JAPAN

Dining etiquette in Japan is tricky. It is considered extremely impolite to pour one's own drink when eating with others—you pour your companion's drink, and your companion pours yours. On the other hand, it is considered normal and nonoffensive to make loud slurping sounds when eating noodles in Japan.

Chopstick etiquette should also be observed by visitors to Japan. The rules for the proper use of chopsticks are many. Never use chopsticks to point at somebody, and do not leave the chopsticks standing up out of the food.

Improper use includes wandering the chopsticks over several foods without decision, which is called *mayoibashi*. The rude act of raking foods into one's already full mouth with chopsticks is disdainfully called *komibashi*. The display of licking the ends of chopsticks is called *neburibashi* and is unforgivable.

On the plus side, there is no tipping at restaurants in Japan.

Course 994: **Strong Medicine?**

> Historical records indicate that the earliest known advocate of a fiber diet was Hippocrates. He urged his fellow countrymen to bake their bread with bran for its "salutary effect on the bowels."
> Ancient Egyptians recommended mixing half an onion with beer foam as a way of warding off death. Radishes were considered a remedy for sexual problems as well.

Chickpeas were believed to be a powerful aphrodisiac, especially for men. Romans fed them to their stallions.

> Dioscorides, a Greek physician in the first century A.D., recorded several medicinal uses of onions. The Greeks used onions to fortify their athletes for the Olympic Games. Before competition, athletes would consume many pounds of onions and drink onion juice. They also rubbed onions on their bodies in preparation.
> The Aztecs believed that cacao came from heaven and that eating it gives people wisdom. They drank it from goblets made of gold.

The custom of serving a slice of lemon with fish dates back to the Middle Ages. It was believed that if a person accidentally swallowed a fish bone, the lemon juice would dissolve it.

> In Ecuador, there is a broth called *caldo de pata,* containing chunks of boiled cow hooves. It is is considered a delicacy by locals and believed by hopeful men to increase virility.
> Ketchup was once used as a medicine in the United States. In the 1830s it was sold as Dr. Miles's Compound Extract of Tomato.
> Green tea has 50 percent more vitamin C than black tea.

The liquid inside young coconuts can be used as a substitute for blood plasma in an emergency. This was discovered by doctors in Fiji during World War II.

The Pop Heard Round the World

The Aztec Indians used popcorn as decoration for ceremonial headdresses, necklaces, and ornaments on statues of their gods. About 1612, early French explorers reported that the Iroquois popped popcorn in a pottery vessel with heated sand and used it to make popcorn soup.

A hundred years later, housewives in Colonial America served popcorn with sugar and cream for breakfast, making popcorn the first "puffed" breakfast cereal eaten by Europeans. Nevertheless, popcorn was banned at most movie theaters in the 1920s because it was considered just too noisy, given that the films were silent.

Course 999: Any Way You Slice It

> The first known pizza shop, Port 'Alba in Naples, opened in 1830 and is still open today. Gennaro Lombardi opened the first pizzeria in North America in 1905 at 53⅓ Spring Street in New York City.
> In order to get the Naples Pizza Association seal of approval, pizza must meet stringent requirements. It must have a thin crust and be made of Italian

flour. The sauce must be made from scratch, with fresh, not dried, basil. The mozzarella must be snow white, made in Italy, and worked by hand—for a knife can cause a metallic flavor in the cheese. Plus the pizza cannot ever, under any circumstances, exceed 12 inches in diameter.

According to purist Italian chefs, ingredients that should never appear on an authentic Italian pizza include bell pepper, pepperoni, or chicken.

> In Australia, the #1 topping for pizza is eggs. In Chile, the favorite topping is mussels and clams. In the United States, it's pepperoni.
> In Eastern Europe, ketchup is often used on pizza as a condiment. In Iceland, Domino's Pizza has a reindeer sausage pie on its menu.
> *Okonomiyaki* is considered to be Japan's answer to pizza. It consists of a potpourri of grilled vegetables, noodles, and meat or seafood placed between two pancakelike layers of fried batter.

Final Exam

1. Americans eat more Kraft macaroni-and-cheese packaged dinners than any other nationality in the world.

True or False?

2. The oldest registered food trademark still in use in the United States is the infant girl seen on all Gerber's baby food jars.

True or False?

3. Dried bananas have only a fraction of the food value of fresh bananas.

True or False?

4. If you were to rub garlic on the heel of your foot, it would be absorbed by the pores and eventually show up on your breath.

True or False?

5. In ancient Rome, it was considered a sacred obligation to eat the flesh of a woodpecker.

True or False?

6. Lemons contain more sugar than strawberries.

True or False?

7. Of all the potatoes grown in the United States, over 80 percent are used to make potato chips.

True or False?

8. Removing an olive pit will enhance the flavor of the olive.

True or False?

9. Half the foods eaten throughout the world today were developed by farmers in France.

True or False?

10. The fortune cookie was invented over 3,000 years ago, during the Chinese Ming Dynasty, as a special treat for the imperial family, by a chef who was also the official court astrologer.

True or False?

ANSWERS

1. FALSE. Canadians eat more.

2. FALSE. It's the red devil on cans of Underwood's deviled ham, and it dates back to 1886.

3. FALSE. They're actually four times as nutritious as fresh bananas.

4. TRUE. But there is no research to indicate that if you eat garlic, the smell will show up on your feet.

5. FALSE. Actually, it was a sin.

6. TRUE.

7. FALSE. Only 8 percent are used. Special varieties referred to as "chipping potatoes" are grown for this purpose.

8. FALSE. It will diminish it.

9. FALSE. Half were developed by farmers in the Andes mountains, who first cultivated peanuts, potatoes, beans, squash, pineapples, peppers, tomatoes, etc.

10. FALSE. It was invented in 1916 by George Jung, a Los Angeles noodle maker.

About the Editors

JOE EDELMAN

The Useless-Infomaster is creator of the world-famous Web site, www.UselessKnowledge.com. Involved with the "Net" since 1995, Joe was part of the original management team that worked to take VerticalNet, Inc., from a B2B start-up, through a 1999 IPO and on to become the leading developer of online business communities and solutions.

His on-line brainchild has been applauded in *Time* magazine, TBS Superstation, *Maxim, Seventeen, PC World, ESPN: The Magazine, Muscle and Fitness*, plus Yahoo Internet Life Magazine.

Joe is also an award winning advertising, fashion, and editorial photographer. His work can be seen at www.JoeEdelman.com, and his studio is based in the Philadelphia Metro area.

DAVID SAMSON

David (aka www.FunnyGuy.com) has written fifteen books including titles in humor, psychology, fitness, business, and celebrity areas. His work has been featured in *People, Penthouse, Mademoiselle, Cosmopolitan, USA Today*, and seen on *David Letterman, The Today Show, Rosie O'Donnell, Regis and Kathy Lee, Geraldo Rivera, Politically Incorrect, ABC Prime Time Live, Comedy Central, Entertainment Tonight, Donahue*, and *Larry King*.

In a previous lifetime, David was a senior creative executive at some of America's most prestigious advertising agencies, winning his fair share of awards. Today, he is a highly sought after corporate speaker and consultant specializing in advertising, marketing, and motivation. David is a member of the National Speakers Association but is often mistaken for Neil Diamond.